HEROIC
STORIES

KINGFISHER
An imprint of Kingfisher Publications Plc
New Penderel House, 283-288 High Holborn
London WC1V 7HZ
www.kingfisherpub.com

Originally published as *True Stories* by Kingfisher 1994
This edition published by Kingfisher 2005
2 4 6 8 10 9 7 5 3 1

A CIP catalogue record for this book is available from the British Library

ISBN-13: 978 0 7534 1251 0
ISBN-10: 0 7534 1251 9

Printed in India
1TR/THOM/MA/80Vol-18/F

HEROIC
STORIES

CHOSEN BY
ANTHONY MASTERS

ILLUSTRATED BY
CHRIS MOLAN

KINGFISHER

CONTENTS

FOREWORD

ANTHONY MASTERS

T HERE ARE MANY different types of courage, and in this book I am hoping that you will meet many of them. The courage needed to face a gale in mid-Atlantic, for instance, is very different from that required to endure years in solitary confinement. Working with the poor is a stark contrast to facing death or battling a physical handicap, very different from the dangerous and unpredictable task of exploration. Some of the people in *True Stories* deliberately sought out danger and adventure like Charles Lindbergh the aviator, Chris Bonington the climber, or Clare Francis the lone sailor; whilst others, such as Colonel Archibald Gracie on the *Titanic*, Dian Fossey protecting her gorillas in Africa, Pauline Cutting in the Palestinian refugee camps, Pat Reid in Colditz, and Anne Frank hiding from the Nazis in occupied Amsterdam, behaved heroically when thrown by chance into difficult circumstances.

Some, however, from an early age, had either a vocation or a passionate sense of destiny, like Mother Teresa in India, Nelson Mandela in South Africa, Martin Luther King in America, and Neil Armstrong, Michael Collins and Edwin E. Aldrin Junior, who were the first men on the moon. There are also those who stayed at home, campaigning for the freedom of others, like Peggy Say, Terry Anderson's sister, who fought so vigorously for the release of America's longest-held hostage. Finally, no one must forget the courage shown by scientists such as Louis Pasteur and engineers of the calibre of Brunel.

The true stories in this book are told in all kinds of different ways, ranging from diaries kept as the action unfolded, autobiographies that had the benefit of hindsight and re-evaluation, biographies that bring a more objective view and even a transcript of sound montage that vividly brings to life the Apollo 11 spacecraft landing.

Some years ago I became the biographer of Hannah Senesh, a young Jewish girl who emigrated to Palestine from Hungary in 1939 and who was one of a team who parachuted back into her homeland on a virtual suicide mission in 1943. Her goal was to help set up escape routes for Jews fleeing from Nazi persecution. Through her family and friends and her own diaries, I grew to respect and understand the true story of Hannah Senesh's selfless determination and courage, some of which is encapsulated in the following extract from her diary:

"I've had a shattering week. I was suddenly struck by the idea of going to Hungary. I feel I must be there during these days in order to help organise youth immigration, and also to bring my mother out. Although I'm quite aware how absurd the idea is, it still seems both feasible and necessary to me, so I'll get to work on it and carry it through."

The words are almost mundane, but Hannah followed through her plans until a Nazi firing squad put an abrupt end to them. Her courage was long-term, clear-minded and absolute.

TEST FLIGHT DRAMA

CHARLES LINDBERGH

from Autobiography of Values

Charles A. Lindbergh (1902-1974) was the greatest aviator in history. He made the first solo transatlantic flight in his aeroplane The Spirit of St Louis *from New York to Paris, on May 20, 1927. Always an adventurer, Lindbergh was also philosophical and able to analyse how the mind responds to danger and panic. Here he describes how, in 1925, he bailed out of a biplane that was about to crash.*

I LEARNED HOW QUICKLY I could fragment or unify during the tests of a single-engine biplane at Lambert Field in the summer of 1925. It was a new design, locally built, the only one of its kind. Its plywood fuselage was a little on the short and stubby side. I had approached that plane while it was still under construction, through a planning of the mind: I would inspect it thoroughly; I would get a rough "feel" while taxiing, hold the wheels close to the ground while I tried out the controls, cut the throttle if anything went wrong – fortunately, Lambert Field was big and smooth. If I was well satisfied with take-off and response, I would climb slowly to two or three thousand feet, which would give me plenty of altitude for using my parachute in an emergency, put the plane through some wing-tip stalls, and then consider acrobatics.

At the end of that test flight, I experienced unity and fragmentation pulsing back and forth in extraordinarily quick succession. I climbed to an altitude of twenty-five hundred feet, made several wingovers and banks, tested the controls at increasing angles of attack, power on, power off. Then I tried spinning; and on the fourth attempt found myself trapped in a lunging left tailspin. Reversing the stick and rudder had no effect.

Mind, senses, body jerked to tension. I had never before flown a plane that refused any response to its controls; and I had never been in a spin so violent and lunging, and so flat. The ground whirled erratically. Ideas inside my head were whirling, too. Maybe the slipstream would bring more pressure on control surfaces. I opened the throttle. My hand was not conscious of its movement, but my ears heard the engine howling through other sensations.

The buck and plunge of the plane continued, carrying my body through its wild convulsions. The ground twisted upward toward my eyes. Muscles reported the rudder jammed full right and the stick strained to the forward corner of the cockpit. I reversed ailerons, closed the throttle, and tried another burst of power.

The lunging continued. Fields and houses grew tremendous and the ground terribly close. Fingers snapped open the safety belt. Hands grasped cowlings. Legs shoved and flexed in piston actions. "I" – mind and senses and body as a unit – plunged out beyond the confines of the cockpit. Tug on shoulders – turn of body – harness hugging – canopy billowing, white on blue. I swung like the bob of a pendulum, barely two hundred feet from the bottom of earth's air. Body twists – feet hit ground -- parachute drags me with the wind.

I reached for the shroud lines, but only one of my arms responded. I became conscious of dull pain. Several men ran up and caught hold of my parachute. I found myself lying in a potato patch. When I got onto my feet, I started to walk slowly in the direction of the crashed plane. People from the village came crowding about. Pain began stabbing, cutting through my shoulder. I realized that my left hand was holding my right arm, which stuck out in a rigid, unnatural position. I climbed slowly into the back seat of an automobile and started the trip to a hospital.

Pain makes you realize the juxtaposition of unity and diversity within the body, bringing out first one and then the other according to circumstance. Obviously, my shoulder was not my mind. My mind was not hurt. The shoulder joint had been injured while acting without the mind's knowledge or consent. It was responsible for its own troubles. My mind should arrange for its cure, and direct its care, and at the same time maintain an intellectual position above corruption by the flesh. But each jolt on the road decreased mental objectivity. My shoulder kept jabbing into thought and all the senses until it forced the elements of existence to unify again, to agree that, for the time being, the shoulder's pain was *me* and that little else mattered in my personal welfare.

Later in 1929, Lindbergh made the most daring of landings in his search for knowledge.

Man has only begun to scratch his record on the stone pages of geology. Marks of more than a hundred thousand years ago are scarce – bits of chipped flint, a few fragments of bone. We have found none in the Western Hemisphere. At the Grand Canyon the only human marks I saw lay on the surface of the earth, waiting to be covered by sediments of time: a surfaced road, a sheep corral, a big hotel on the canyon rim. I once stayed in that hotel. It was prosperous, well kept, its parlours and corridors open with hospitality. I watched the waiters serving food at silver-garnished tables, listened to chattering guests and strains of music in the background. I amused myself by speculating on whether the hotel itself would eventually be buried under layers of rock, and if so, what fragments would be left to communicate life to an archaeologist's eye. A few hours earlier I had flown over an abandoned Indian dwelling, its stones already merging with the drifted sand. Who could reconstruct the life once housed in those roofless walls?

There was the "now" of the hotel. There was the "past"

of the Indian dwelling, so distant to aviation's era, so recent in geological time. There were the fossils in the rocks beneath me, reaching back to ages beyond human memory. The effects of prolificacy, competition, survival and progressively advancing weapons were evident, even in the fragments that remained. Prolificacy, strife, survival – these three basic elements of life I encountered wherever I combined archaeology with aviation.

In the summer of 1929 my wife and I explored areas of New Mexico and Arizona for signs of ancient men. We were working with the archaeological division of the Carnegie Institution of Washington, flying an open-cockpit Curtiss Falcon biplane.

Under certain angles of light, old ruins can be seen from an airplane, but you might walk across them on the ground without knowing they existed. Walls, rain-washed to the level of the earth, may appear as crisscross lines to the aviator's eye, and changed shades of vegetation show where people dug their pits and dumped their refuse thousands of years ago. Our mission was to photograph ancient ruins, and to map their exact position so that ground expeditions could then locate and explore them. We flew back and forth over mountains, plains, plateaus, and desert edges, sometimes climbing high to select an interesting valley, sometimes flying below a cliff rim while we watched for caves and piled-up rocks. From our altitude we saw the earth's great contours, an entire desert, the branching sources of a river, a rounding ridge of mountains that looked like a huge volcano's rim. Closer to the ground we could see details that helped us separate natural formations from those of men.

Approaching a line of cliffs in Arizona, with sheer walls rising from the ground below, I opened my throttle to clear the plateau on top. Cliff edges contrasted with their valley somewhat as land contrasts with sea. To the left a peninsula jutted out like the state of Florida on a chart, long, narrow-necked before bulging. Our eyes caught,

vaguely, but definitely etched upon its surface, the familiar lines that mark a ruined Peublo city. It was not listed in archaeological records, but it was by far the largest we had seen. As we banked to take photographs I wondered what enemies had forced those ancient people to a place so high and far from water. How could attacking warriors have advanced through a neck so narrow, or scaled walls so sheer? What had caused the abandonment of a large, well-fortified city? Was it disease? Starvation? A battle line that did not hold? All three? My mind skipped across centuries to imagine a thriving culture: square adobe houses, with wooden rafters, built in several tiers; men and women with their brown-skinned, black-haired children. We knew what they had looked like, and the kind of dwellings they lived in, because we had spent a night in Canyon de Chelly, in northeastern Arizona. We had even come in contact with these people's problems of survival.

On a previous exploration we had flown down the Canyon de Chelly, searching for cliff houses hidden under shelves and behind ledges in the walls. Some distance from the mouth of the canyon, near what are called the "White House" ruins, an archaeological expedition was encamped. Since we could not land on the stony river bed, we had settled for merely waving to its staff as we passed. But about a quarter of a mile upstream from the camp we saw an Indian trail, with ladders and notches, threading down the precipitous left wall. The tableland above the canyon was fairly level. It was only lightly spotted with prairie-dog holes, cactus, and brush. Why not pay the archaeologists a visit? We selected a clear stretch of ground that lay into the wind and landed – bumping over fist-size stones and hummocks.

It was taking a chance to leave our plane on that mesa all night, but the sky showed no indication of a storm and we eagerly wanted to see at close range some of the ruins we were photographing – to touch the earth, pick up the shards, and talk to scientists who worked with screen and shovel. We dug holes for the Falcon's wheels and tail skid, roped its wings to sturdy bushes, and started out for the camp. There was no sign of recent travel on the footpath that angled steeply over a cliff edge, yet it was not difficult to follow. It took us along rock ledges and through narrow crevices toward the canyon floor. The weathered wood.of the pole ladders, though broken in places, was still firm enough to hold our weight.

"You landed on the mesa? But how did you get down?" Members of the archaeological expedition did not know a trail existed, although they had walked back and forth past its lower entrance for many weeks. Under the White House, isolated by the canyon's red and perpendicular walls, and somehow set in a professorial atmosphere of centuries past, we described our flights and observations. We realized that in our generation the airplane had given eyes of birds to the minds of men.

SISTER TO THE POOR

PATRICIA REILLY GIFF

from Mother Teresa: Sister to the Poor

Agnes Gonxha Bojaxhiu (or Mother Teresa) was a missionary whose name became known throughout the world as a result of her work with the poor and homeless in India. Mother Teresa was born in 1910 in Skopje in the Former Yugoslav Republic of Macedonia and became a nun at the age of eighteen. For many years she taught in a school in Calcutta, but after seeing the terrible conditions in which many of the city's poorest people lived, she felt compelled to devote her life to caring for them. Mother Teresa died in 1997.

SEPTEMBER 1946 CAME. It was time for Sister Teresa's retreat. Thirty-six years old now, she had made this yearly visit to Darjeeling many times. Freed from her teaching duties, she would spend several days there, praying, thinking in silence. It was a time she loved.

This September she boarded the night train. As always her thoughts were of the poor, the sick, the dying, the children. As the dusty train carried her north, she could picture the peace of St Mary's. At the same time, she could see the slums of Moti Jheel, the bustee that was named Pearl Lake after a dirty pond that lay in that area.

Moti Jheel was outside her window, but it seemed a million miles away.

"I must do something," she kept telling herself.

Then suddenly she knew.

For years she had been saying to herself that she knew where she belonged. Every time she looked out the window. Every time she stepped into Moti Jheel.

But she hadn't known how to get there.

Now, on the dusty night train, she felt that God was calling her again. He was telling her that the people outside needed her, that they would not come behind the convent walls to her. She had to go out to them.

She called this message "a call within a call." It was not a vision from God, but a strong sense of knowing what He wanted.

She would still be a sister, but a sister in a different way.

The message was crystal clear. "I was to give up even Loreto where I was very happy," she said, "and go out in the streets. I heard the call to give up all and follow Christ into the slums to serve him among the poorest of the poor."

She felt that "It was an order. I was to leave the convent and help the poor while living among them."

But getting outside was not to be easy. She went first to a priest, a spiritual adviser. He promised he would talk to the Archbishop of Calcutta.

The Archbishop was worried. How could he send this woman outside? In addition to the poverty, religious problems were still causing fighting in Calcutta. Sister Teresa was a Western woman. Who knew what the people might do to her?

He told her that she had to wait a year before any decision would be made.

But the faith and determination that had always been hers never wavered.

It had brought her all the way from Skopje. It had made her give up her family, her friends. It had taken her to Ireland, a place she could hardly remember anymore.

A year later she asked again. By now the Archbishop had discussed her request with priests and other people in Calcutta. He had had time to think about what she wanted to do. He agreed to her plan, provided she could get permission from her order.

The General Superior of the Loreto Sisters, Mother Gertrude, gave Sister Teresa her blessing. She wrote, "If God is calling you, I give you permission with all my heart."

The permission was given for just a year – a time of trial.

Now that the time had come, Sister Teresa felt the terrible pain of separation from her sisters.

"To leave Loreto was much more difficult than to leave my family and country to enter religious life," she said later. "Loreto, my spiritual training, my work, meant everything to me."

On August 16, 1948, she took off the black veil and the habit of the Loreto Order.

She put on a simple white cotton sari, the dress of Indian women. This sari had three stripes of blue. It was cheap and familiar to the poor. She pinned a small cross to her left shoulder, and slipped into open sandals.

It was the day to leave.

Her students and the sisters were in tears. She fought back tears too as, one by one, they hugged her and the children sang songs of farewell.

Then she walked out of the gates of St Mary's.

Sister Teresa had one more stop before she reached the streets of Calcutta. That stop was Patna ("Potna"), a city 240 miles away. Patna and the Medical Mission Sisters at Holy Family Hospital.

The sisters there had agreed to help Sister Teresa learn as much as she could about sickness in a short period of time.

She was given a tiny room in the hospital. From there it was just a few steps to the patients. She learned how to give an injection. She learned how to measure medicine. She washed the children and the old people and held the hands of people in pain. She even delivered a baby.

Whenever there were a few minutes, she asked questions. The sisters were glad to answer.

They knew about the types of illnesses Sister Teresa would meet in the bustees of Calcutta, diseases that had mostly disappeared in Western countries.

There was leprosy. There were intestinal worms. There were bone-softening diseases from lack of vitamins and good food.

The sisters knew the kinds of first aid that would be helpful for Sister Teresa to use.

In a few months they filled Sister's head with all the practical advice they could.

Sister Teresa confided in them. She told of her hopes for a new group of sisters, who would work with the poorest of the poor – the people of Calcutta. These sisters would go out to the people instead of staying behind walls.

She was determined that they would live like the poor. They would wear the simple white sari with the blue border. They'd eat the same food; just rice with a little salt for seasoning.

Rice and salt? The sisters were shocked. The new sisters would quickly become as sick as the poor of India on such a diet. They told Sister Teresa that the people who worked with the poor had to be strong. They needed to be well fed and well rested.

In the years to come, Sister Teresa would remember this advice and use it.

By this time it was nearly Christmas. Sister Teresa was ready to begin her new life.

She arrived back in Calcutta on December 1, 1948. She had five rupees – worth less than a dollar – in her pocket.

She went straight to Moti Jheel. The stench of the bustee

hit her in the face. She threaded her way around huge piles of human waste mixed with old corn husks. She watched the children playing on this heap of waste, the rats running back and forth, the beggars looking for a little morsel of corn to eat.

Faced with the filth, the sickness, the hunger, the numbers of people lying in the streets, where would she begin?

She began with the children.

In the middle of the bustee she found an open spot between the huts. She smoothed down a caked patch of earth and began to trace the Bengali letters with a small stick.

One by one, the slum children came to see what she was

21

doing. At first there were only a few, but in no time there were about thirty children. They crouched on the ground beside her.

Then she began to teach them about cleanliness. Before she began the alphabet lesson each day, she washed them with soap and water.

What a strange experience it was for them! They had hardly ever washed. Most of them had never even seen a piece of soap.

Some of her old friends from St Mary's heard about what she was doing and came to see her. They brought things for the school with them – paper, chairs, and, more exciting, bars of soap. Sister Teresa gave the soap to the children as prizes.

She managed to get some milk, too. It was just enough to give the children a drink at lunchtime.

After school was over for the day, she would scurry around the Moti Jheel and Til-Jala ("Teel-Jella") bustees. Someone gave her some medical supplies so she could set up a dispensary – a place to work with the sick, to give out medicine. She cleaned the sick and cared for them, bandaging them when she could get bandages. She used the knowledge she had gained and pure common sense as well.

Sometimes she begged for scraps of food at the door of the church so she could feed one or two starving people. At the same time, she continued to live the life of a sister.

Up at four-thirty in the morning, she attended Mass and received Communion. She said her prayers with the Little Sisters of the Poor, who were also working in Calcutta. She continued to pray as she taught and worked with the sick and the dying, long into the evening hours.

But for every beggar who sipped the water she brought, there were thousands more who were thirsty. For every starving man who received a scrap of food from her, there were dozens more at her feet who held their hands up for something.

For every child she taught, there were untold numbers who would never learn to read and write.

People followed her in the streets, begging for help. Those who couldn't walk clutched at her feet and the bottom of her sari.

The work she had started was endless. She was tired; every part of her ached.

She remembered the silence of Loreto that she loved, the peace. She remembered that the Mother Superior had told

her that she was loved, that she could come back to the Sisters of Loreto. She wrote what she felt:

Today I learned a good lesson. The poverty of the poor is so hard. When I was going and going till my legs and arms were paining, I was thinking how they have to suffer to get food and shelter. Then the comfort of Loreto came to tempt, but of my own free choice, my God, and out of love for You, I desire to remain. Give me courage.

She was determined. She would not stop. Instead of thinking of the crowds, the thousands, she thought of the one – the one closest, the one she was helping.

Asked how she was able to do it, how she was able to stand the terrible smell of human waste and vomit, the sickness, the dying, she said that every time she worked with someone ill, she felt as if she were meeting God.

Every time she gave someone a cup of water, she was giving it to the Lord; every time she found a scrap of food for someone, she was finding it for Him.

"We meet the Lord who hungers and thirsts in the poor," she said, "and the poor could be you or I or any person."

Up to this time she had been staying with the Little Sisters of the Poor. She wanted to be closer to Moti Jheel, closer to the people she was helping.

A priest friend helped her find a place – the upstairs room of a house owned by a Catholic teacher, Michael Gomes. Mr Gomes not only gave her the room; he gave it to her without rent, and he made sure there was enough food for her to eat. She added a small chair, a box for a desk, and hung a picture of the Blessed Mother on the wall.

Then more help arrived for the poor in the form of a small, pretty Bengali girl named Shubashini Das ("Shu-ba-shi-nee").

Shubashini had been one of Sister Teresa's pupils at St Mary's. Now she had graduated. She was there to help, there to stay.

24

Sister Teresa warned her that it would not be easy. In fact it would be terribly hard. Remembering the sisters' advice at Patna, she told Shubashini that she would have enough to eat – but just enough. She would have to give up her lovely saris, her home, her family. She would have to give them up willingly. . . and with love.

The shy Shubashini, smaller even than Sister Teresa, nodded. She became Sister Teresa's first postulant. She put on the plain white sari that cost about a dollar. She pinned the small crucifix to her left shoulder, and she took a new name.

Shubashini was now Sister Agnes, Agnes in honour of Sister Teresa's own baptismal name. Next came the new Sister Gertrude, and Sister Bernard, and Sister Frederick.

They would soon learn that Sister Teresa was fiercely determined to reach out to the poor. They would live like the poor; otherwise she would never be able to face them. There would be no fans in the stifling hot rooms, no extra food, no extra rest.

From morning to night they would work with the poor. As a matter of fact, instead of the usual three vows a nun takes – poverty, chastity, and obedience – they would take four. This fourth one would be a promise to serve the poorest of the poor.

On October 7, 1950, the Archbishop said the first Mass at the Gomes house. Sister Teresa was given permission to go on with the work. It was the beginning of the order of sisters she had hoped for. She called them the Missionaries of Charity. . . and from then on she would be called Mother.

RESCUE ON THE EIGER

CHRIS BONINGTON

from I Chose to Climb

Chris Bonington is a mountaineer, photographer, adventure journalist and expedition organiser. He began climbing as a schoolboy and his most spectacular feat has been an Everest expedition. The danger such mountaineers face is evoked vividly in this account of a rescue on the notorious Eiger North Wall.

WE SAW TWO CLIMBERS coming up towards us. The one in front shouted something in German – I couldn't understand what.

"We're English," we shouted.

"Two of your comrades are injured," he replied. "Will you help us to rescue them?"

Of course we agreed and turned back up the slope. At this stage we didn't know just what had happened. The previous day, through a telescope at Alpiglen, we had seen two climbers moving very slowly across the Second Ice-field; we didn't know who they were.

We only heard the full story when we got back down. The pair were Brian Nally and Barry Brewster, two climbers from Southern England. I had met Barry once before; he was a student at Bangor University – one of their tigers. I was impressed, and a little frightened, by his intense seriousness as he talked about climbing. He had done all the hardest routes in Wales, climbing many of them in tricounis just to improve his technique. His experience on ice was limited: he had had several seasons in Chamonix, but, like most British climbers, had tended to do rock routes. Brian Nally, a house painter from London, was the ice specialist of the party. The previous year he had made the first British ascent of the North Face of the Matterhorn with Tom Carruthers, a Glasgow climber. Before going on the face, they had agreed that Brewster should be the rock expert, while Nally should take the lead on the ice-fields. In Nally's words – "he was the brains of the team – I the navvy."

They set out just twenty-four hours before us, bivouacked in the Swallow's Nest and, like us, were soaked to the skin. That morning they started out up the side of the First Ice-field, but instead of going into the Ice Hose, they followed Heinrich Harrer's description from the back of his book, *The White Spider*, and attempted the wall, about a hundred feet to its left. In doing this they lost the route and wasted several hours. As a result it was getting on for midday when they reached the Second Ice-field. Here they decided to cut steps diagonally across it, and so their progress was slow.

It was four o'clock when they reached the end of the ice-field; the stone-fall was by now violent as the afternoon sun loosened the rock in the upper part of the face. Looking up at the Eiger, it is difficult to get any idea of scale, the top is so foreshortened, but the entire upper 2,000 feet of the Eigerwand are in the shape of a huge amphitheatre round the White Spider. Every stone that falls inevitably goes into the Spider, which then acts as a funnel, concentrating the bombardment down the centre of the face on to the Flat Iron. This place is a death trap after midday.

Barry Brewster took over the lead at the foot of a rock pitch – the start of the Flat Iron.

"There's a pitch of V Sup. up here," he remarked, as he took off his crampons.

He ran out about eighty feet of rope, and clipped into a couple of pegs. Nally, who was belayed to a ring peg at the top of the ice-field heard him shout –

"Stones!"

Brian ducked into the rock instinctively, for he was now hardened to the constant bombardment that they had experienced from the start of the Second Ice-Field.

Suddenly, the dark shape of a body came hurtling down. Both peg runners were pulled out by the force of the fall, and Nally was only just able to hold the rope – the peg to which he was belayed bent to a frightening angle. The rope held, and Barry was lying suspended on the end of it on the steep ice a hundred feet below. When Nally reached him, having secured the rope to the peg, Barry was unconscious. Brian Nally then did everything that anyone could have done in the circumstances. He cut out a ledge for his friend – no easy matter in hard ice, with the stones continuously whistling down – gave the injured man his crash hat, wrapped him up in all the available spare clothes and then settled down for the night; his second in wet clothes.

The following morning we learnt of the accident, and turned back up the ice slope. Don led out the first pitch, slowly cutting steps – it was no good moving fast now, we had to have a line of large steps on which to retreat with an injured man.

"I think I can see someone," Don called down. "Look, at the top of the ice-field."

I could just discern a small red figure moving slowly along the top.

"Stop where you are," shouted Don. "We'll come up to you."

He didn't reply, but took no notice and continued for

thirty feet or so; then he stopped on a small spur, and seemed to be lying down. This gave us some idea of the vast scale of the face, of the distance we had to cover to reach him – he was just a minute blob of colour in the dull grey of plunging rock and gleam of ice.

We were now getting used to the sound of falling stones which were coming down the whole time: a high-pitched whistle, then a thud as they hit the ice around us and bounded on down the face.

"It's as good as a war film," remarked Don, after a particularly bad bombardment.

But then we heard a deeper sound – it seemed to fill the wall with its wild keen. I looked across and saw the tiny figure of a man shoot down the ice into space. It was like being hit hard in the stomach – I just hugged the ice and swore over and over again – then got a grip of myself – became aware of the danger we were in, of the man who was still alive at the end of the ice-field – the little red blob of colour was still there; it must have been the injured man who had fallen.

We shall never know exactly what happened, but probably Brewster had been swept from his perch by stonefall. Mercifully, he was dead when he fell, for Nally had been with him when he died early that morning.

If he hadn't died, I am not sure what we could have done to bring him down. Although fourteen Swiss Guides had come as far as the Gallery Window, it is doubtful if they would have crossed the ice-fields, and anyway, it would not have been justifiable. Nally told us that Brewster was paralysed below the waist, probably with a broken back; in trying to carry him back we should almost certainly have killed him. To carry him, we should have needed at least eight people, and with such a number and the time it would have all taken, someone else would inevitably have been hit by stones.

We could certainly rescue the remaining climber, however, so Don and I continued cutting across the ice-field. It wasn't so bad while you were actually moving – your attention was completely taken up with the job in hand – but it was a different matter on the stances; you then had sufficient time to wonder about the chances of being hit by stones, to notice that the weather was closing in. The sky was now completely overcast; wisps of grey mist were reaching round the side of the face. I pressed myself against the ice, tried to vanish under the protective cover of my crash hat, to present as small a target as possible; stones whistled and landed all round me: one bounced off my helmet, another hit my shoulder – is anything broken? I worked my arm up and down – it felt numb but I could move my fingers – just a bruise, nothing more. And so it went on –

"Come on, Chris."

I left the ice peg in place for our retreat, and hurried to join Don. I could see the line of the other party's steps just above us – they had been partly washed away by the streams of water pouring down the ice, and, anyway, seemed to wander haphazardly across the face.

"It's no good following their line," Don remarked. "It'd be too difficult getting back along it. We must cut across in a dead straight line."

Pitch followed pitch – it just never seemed to end; all this time Nally was lying inert on the small spur of rock. I wondered if he also was injured, whether he would be able to help himself on the way back. Don and I now felt very much on our own, for the two Swiss Guides had vanished – there was no one else on the face and I couldn't help wondering what would happen to us if we were hit by stones.

One last rope length and I found myself only a few feet from Nally; I had run out the full length of rope, so turned round to tell Don to come up so that he could lead the last few feet.

"It's all right," Nally called out. "I can come over to you."

31

I had never met Brian Nally before. At first glance he seemed unaffected by his ordeal. He was wearing a red duvet that clung wetly to him, and he moved slowly, methodically, as he cut steps across to me. Round his neck, in a tangle of knitting, was his climbing rope; an end of it trailed behind him. His features were heavy with fatigue. He had a look of simplicity, yet in his eyes there was a wildness.

"Are you going to the top? Can I tie on to you?" he asked.

My nerves, already stretched, exploded.

"We've come to get you down, you fool."

"But why not go on up, now that you've come this far."

past twenty years, he led down to the left to the brink of a sheer drop. Just a hundred and fifty feet below was the end of the Hinterstoisser Traverse – if only Hinterstoisser and his companions, who discovered this line in 1936, and in doing so, the key to the Eiger, had found this way down they would have been alive today; instead they tried to get back across the traverse, having failed to leave a rope in place behind them to safeguard their retreat. Without it, the traverse was impassable and they lost their lives in trying to abseil straight down the sheer wall below it.

Once down by the side of the traverse, we began to feel more safe, though I didn't relax till we reached the Stollenloch Window, where a reception party was waiting. We were pulled through the window, blinded by the flash bulbs of press cameras, and the whole ghastly nightmare reached its climax.

Glossary of mountaineering terms:
tricounis metal spikes fixed to climbing boots to help grip
bivouack spend the night outside
belay fix the end of a climbing rope
piton iron peg to which a rope may be attached
abseil a technique for letting oneself down a rock face using a double rope
traverse a passage across the face of a rock

"Your friend is dead! Do you realise that? We're taking you down."

It was only then that I realised how shocked he was, how misplaced my anger. He was like an automaton, did what you told him, but was incapable of thinking.

"We'll have to put you in the middle, between us. We'll use your rope. Give it to me."

I spent the next twenty minutes untangling the rope – it was knotted as only three hundred feet of nylon can be. Each knot had to be undone separately, the rope was sodden, it numbed and cut my hands, but at least I was doing something. Don, a hundred and fifty feet below, was in the line of some of the worst stone-fall. All he could do was to wait patiently and watch the storm gather about our heads.

At last the rope was untangled. I tied Brian into the middle and he started back towards Don. Our progress was painfully slow – most of the steps had again been washed away by streams of water pouring down the ice – and stones were still coming down the whole time. Brian had given his crash hat to Brewster; a stone hit his head with a dull thud, he teetered backwards, and I grabbed his arm, pulling him back into the ice. He shook his head and seemed all right, or, at least, no more shocked than before.

At the end of the ice-field the storm broke: there was a deafening blast of thunder followed by a torrent of hail. Like a river in spate, it completely covered us, tore at us with steadily increasing force. We were all suspended from the same ice piton which was submitted to a seemingly impossible strain. Then, as suddenly as it started, the storm stopped.

"Let's get a move on," Don shouted, "before it starts again."

We abseiled carefully down the Ice Hose, and then Don demonstrated yet again his genius as a mountaineer. Instead of branching back right, the way we had come up, the way used as a line of retreat by countless parties in the

"THE BRILLIANT IOLA"

DOROTHY STERLING

from Black Foremothers

American Ida B. Wells-Barnett (1862-1931) was one of the most militant campaigners for black rights in the nineteenth century. She spent only six months of her life in slavery although her father had been a slave for many years. Ida battled all her life to improve the status of African Americans; she campaigned against lynching, was editor of several black newspapers and journals and helped found the National Association of Colored Women, the National Afro-American Council and the National Association for the Advancement of Colored People. One of her first battles with the authorities came in 1884.

"THIS MORNING I STAND face to face with 25 years of life," Ida Wells wrote on her birthday in 1887. "The first ten are so far away as to make those at the beginning indistinct, the next five are remembered as a kind of butterfly existence at school and household duties at home. Within the last ten I have suffered more, learned more, lost more than I ever expect to again. In this last decade I've only begun to live – to know life as a whole with its joys and sorrows."

If this diary entry struck a new note of confidence, it was because Ida Wells had found her vocation. For some time now, she had been writing for black newspapers about the concerns of black people. Her entrance into journalism was triggered by an incident that had occurred three years earlier when she had her first encounter with segregation.

During her childhood, Mississippi – along with most southern states – had had a civil rights law that forbade discrimination in public places; in 1875, a federal Civil Rights Act outlawed segregation all over the country. But by the 1880's, as black voters were driven from the polls and black lawmakers lost their seats in southern legislatures and in Congress, the guarantees of equal rights were fading too. This was brought home forcefully in October 1883 when the Supreme Court ruled that the Civil Rights Act of 1875 was unconstitutional.

"The colored people of the United States feel as if they had been baptized in ice water," wrote T. Thomas Fortune, a prominent journalist. "The Supreme Court now declares that railroad corporations are free to force us into smoking cars or cattle cars; that hotel keepers are free to make us walk the streets at night; that theatre managers can refuse us admittance to their exhibitions." He proposed that black people refuse to move from first-class coaches on trains. If they were beaten or killed for their resistance, it would be for a good cause. "One or two murders growing from this intolerable nuisance would break it up," he wrote.

Six months later, Wells boarded a train in Memphis to return to Woodstock, where she was teaching. Seating herself in the ladies' coach – the first-class car – as she had always done, she began to read. She had had a pleasant weekend and the issue of civil rights was far from her mind. She was brought up short, however, when the conductor, coming by to collect tickets, refused to accept hers. Brusquely, he told her to move to the car ahead, which was reserved for smokers – and blacks. Perhaps recalling Fortune's editorial, she refused to move.

Angered by her defiance, the conductor grabbed her arm

to drag her out – only to have her sink her teeth into the back of his hand. When she braced her feet against the seat in front of her, he went to the baggage car for reinforcements. It took three men to pry Ida Wells loose and to push her out of the coach when the train stopped at the next station. Bruised, the sleeves of her linen duster torn, she tumbled down the steps to the platform while her white fellow passengers stood up and applauded.

Ida Wells returned to Memphis with the sound of that applause echoing in her ears. Her humiliation was more than personal; she could not let the incident pass without protest. The same Supreme Court decision that overturned the Civil Rights Act had advised blacks to apply to state courts for redress of their wrongs. Still secure in her belief in a world where justice would triumph, Wells hired a lawyer and sued the railroad for damages. The case was tried before a judge who had been a Union soldier during the war and was sympathetic to Wells. Finding in her favour, he awarded her $500 in damages.

The case of *Wells* vs. *Chesapeake, Ohio & Southwestern Railroad* was the first to be heard in the South since the demise of the Civil Rights Act. The *Memphis Daily Appeal*, the city's leading newspaper, reported on it with a slurring headline: A DARKY DAMSEL OBTAINS VERDICT FOR DAMAGES AGAINST CHESAPEAKE & OHIO RAILROAD. While the railroad appealed the decision, Wells, flushed with her victory, wrote an account of the case for *The Living Way*, a black church weekly. She had a simple point to make: if you stand up for your rights, you will be able to keep them.

Her article was so favourably received that the editor of *The Living Way* asked for additional contributions, and she began to write a weekly column for the paper over the signature "Iola". "I had observed and thought much about the conditions I had seen in the country schools and churches," she later explained. "I had an instinctive feeling that people who had little or no school training should have something coming into their homes weekly which dealt with their problems in a simple, helpful way. So I wrote in a plain, common-sense way on the things which concerned our people. Knowing that their education was limited, I never used a word of two syllables where one would serve the purpose." At first, her articles were confined to local news: reports of births and deaths, club meetings, reviews of concerts and plays. But soon she ventured to comment on broader issues, detailing "outrages and discrimination," deploring "the contemptuous defamation of black women," and criticizing the "so-called leaders" of her race. Before long, editors in other parts of the country were reading Iola's column and asking her to write for them.

In the 1880s almost two hundred black newspapers were published every week. A handful, most notably T. Thomas Fortune's *New York Age*, were brilliantly written and edited; most were shabby affairs consisting largely of "exchanges" from other black papers and syndicated articles from the white press, with only a page of news and editorials about their local communities. But even the poorest of them served an important function. The white press rarely printed news about black people; only through the black press could they learn about events affecting them and, on occasion, take appropriate action.

By 1886 Ida B. Well's reports on black life in Tennessee were appearing in the most prestigious papers – the *Age*, the Detroit *Plaindealer*, the Indianapolis *Freeman* – as well as in such short-lived publications as the Gate City *Press*

and the Little Rock *Sun*. She wrote a regular column for the *American Baptist*, edited the Home Department of *Our Women and Children*, and contributed to the *AME Church Review*, a monthly magazine. When the Afro-American Press Association held a convention in Louisville, Kentucky, in 1887, "the brilliant Iola" was elected secretary, a position she continued to hold for many years. "I was tickled pink over the attention I received from those veterans of the press," she wrote. "I suppose it was because I was their first woman representative."

Black newspaperwomen were not a new phenomenon. In the 1850s Mary Ann Shadd Cary had founded and edited *The Provincial Freeman*, a weekly that served as a rallying point for black refugees in Canada. Hailed as "one of the best editors in the Province even if she did wear petticoats," she continued to contribute to the press for many years. By the 1880s more than a dozen women were writing for black newspapers, some doing general reporting, but the majority editing women's columns and covering social and school news. Since the days of Mary Ann Cary, however, there had not been a newspaperwoman who wrote as boldly as Ida B. Wells. While admiring her brains and ability, male journalists invariably commented on her appearance, a practice never followed, of course, when discussing men.

The Washington *Bee* described "this remarkable and talented young schoolmarm" as "about four and a half feet high, tolerably well proportioned, and of ready address." "I met Iola," T. Thomas Fortune wrote in 1888:

She has become famous as one of the few of our women who handles a goose quill with diamond point as handily as any of us men. She is rather girlish looking in physique with sharp regular features, penetrating eyes, firm set thin lips and a sweet voice. She stuck to the conference through all the row and gas and seemed to enjoy the experience. If Iola was a man she would be a humming Independent in politics. She has plenty of nerve; she is smart as a steel trap, and she has no sympathy with humbug.

Her writings brought her more fame than cash. She received a dollar a week for her *American Baptist* columns, but other newspapers paid her with extra copies and free subscriptions. She was still teaching in order to support herself when she was asked to join the staff of *Free Speech and Headlight*, a small Memphis weekly. In the summer of 1889, she managed to buy a one-third interest in the paper. Her partners were the Reverend Taylor Nightingale, pastor of the largest black church in Tennessee, and J.L. Fleming, a journalist. With Fleming as business manager and Nightingale in charge of sales, Wells did most of the editorial work. Preaching the doctrines of self-help and thrift that she had been taught at Rust College, she endeavoured to raise the living standards of her readers. Her forceful editorials were critical of both the white and the black establishments. Writing without fear of personal consequences, she was as frank about exposing a black minister who was having an affair with a church member as she was in attacking the poor schools for black children in Memphis. The former brought the members of the preachers' alliance to her office with a threat to denounce *Free Speech* from their pulpits and led to the Reverend Nightingale's withdrawal from the paper. The latter resulted in her dismissal as a teacher.

No matter. Travelling through the Mississippi Valley, in Arkansas, Tennessee, and Mississippi, Wells set out to make *Free Speech* a paying business. With the backing of her father's friend, James Hill, who was postmaster of Vicksburg, and of Isaiah Montgomery, founder of the all-black town of Mound Bayou, she spoke at lodge meetings of the Masons, at church conventions, and at public gatherings, soliciting advertisements as well as subscriptions. After nine months of hard work, the circulation of *Free Speech* had increased from 1,500 to 3,500; within a year she was earning the equivalent of her teacher's salary.

Wherever she went, she found the position of black

people worsening. Hitherto, whites had depended on force and economic pressure to keep black men from voting. But in 1890 Mississippi revised its constitution in order to disfranchise black voters legally. Even Isaiah Montgomery, the lone black member of the constitutional convention, had cast his vote against suffrage – an action for which he was roundly berated in *Free Speech*. Once, Jim Wells had been able to buy a glass of beer in a Holly Springs saloon; Lizzie Wells's church group had held picnics in the local park, and a fête in a public hall. Now, new laws barred blacks from restaurants, parks, and even cemeteries, and required railroads and steamboats to provide "separate but equal" accommodations for the two races.

As other states followed Mississippi's example, segregation was becoming the rule everywhere in the South. Wells received a rude shock when Tennessee's supreme court finally heard the appeal of the Chesapeake, Ohio & Southwestern Railroad in her suit. "We think it is evident that the purpose of the defendant was to harass," the justices wrote. "Her persistence was not in good faith to obtain a comfortable seat for the short ride." Reversing the decision of the lower court, they ordered defendant Wells to pay court costs.

In an unusually emotional outburst, she wrote in her diary:

I had hoped such great things from my suit for my people generally. I have firmly believed all along that the law was on our side and would, when we appealed to it, give us justice. I feel shorn of that belief and utterly discouraged, and just now if it were possible would gather my race in my arms and fly far away with them. God, is there no redress, no peace, no justice in this land for us? Thou hast always fought the battles of the weak and oppressed. Come to my aid and teach me what do do, for I am sorely, bitterly disappointed.

Her discouragement did not last for long. When T. Thomas Fortune proposed the formation of a national Afro-American League that would unite blacks in a fight to secure "the full privileges of citizenship," Ida B. Wells endorsed the proposal, calling it "the grandest idea ever originated by colored men. We have been asleep long enough," she wrote. "Let us march to the front and do battle."

STRUCK BY AN ICEBERG

ARCHIBALD GRACIE

from Titanic – A Survivor's Story

The S.S. Titanic *set sail on her maiden voyage from Southampton to New York on 10 April, 1912. She was the largest ship that had ever been built and was thought to be unsinkable. On the night of April 14-15, the* Titanic *struck an iceberg 800 kilometres south-east of Newfoundland. The collision tore a 91 metre gash in the ship's hull and the ship sank in about 2 hours. The lifeboats held less than half of the approximately 2,200 persons on board. 750 survivors were picked up by the liner* Carpathia. *Archibald Gracie was amongst the last to leave the stricken ship.*

DURING MY SHORT ABSENCE in conducting the ladies to a position of safety, Mr Thayer and Mr Widener had disappeared, but I know not whither. Mr Widener's son, Harry, was probably with them, but Mr Thayer supposed that his young son, Jack, had left the ship in the same boat with his mother. Messrs Thayer and Widener must have gone toward the stern during the short interval of my absence. No one at this point had jumped into the sea. If there had been any, both Clinch Smith and I would have known it. After the water struck the bridge forward there were many who rushed aft, climbed over the rail and jumped, but I never saw one of them.

I was now working with the crew at the davits on the starboard side forward, adjusting them, ready for lowering the Engelhardt boat from the roof of the officers' house to the Boat Deck below. Some one of the crew on the roof, where it was, sang out, "Has any passenger a knife?" I took mine out of my pocket and tossed it to him, saying, "Here is a small penknife, if that will do any good." It appeared to me then that there was more trouble than there ought to have been in removing the canvas cover and cutting the boat loose, and that some means should have been available for doing this without delay. Meantime, four or five long oars were placed aslant against the walls of the officers' house to break the fall of the boat, which was pushed from the roof and slipped with a crash down on the Boat Deck smashing several of the oars. Clinch Smith and I scurried out of the way and stood leaning with our backs against the rail, watching this procedure and feeling anxious lest the boat might have been stove in, or otherwise injured so as to cause her to leak in the water. The account of the junior Marconi operator, Harold S. Bride, supplements mine. "I saw a collapsible boat," he said, "near a funnel, and went over to it. Twelve men were trying to boost it down to the Boat Deck. They were having an awful time. It was the last boat left. I looked at it longingly a few minutes; then I gave a hand and over she went."

About this time I recall that an officer on the roof of the house called down to the crew at this quarter, "Are there any seamen down there among you?" "Aye, aye, sir," was the response, and quite a number left the Boat Deck to assist in what I supposed to have been the cutting loose of the other Engelhardt boat up there on the roof. Again I heard an inquiry for another knife. I thought I recognized the voice of the second officer working up there with the crew. Lightoller has told me, and has written me as well, that "boat A on the starboard side did not leave the ship," while "B was thrown down to the Boat Deck," and was the one on which he and I eventually climbed. The crew had thrown the Engelhardt boat to the deck, but I did not understand why they were so long about launching it, unless they were waiting to cut the other one loose and launch them both at the same time. Two young men of the crew, nice looking, dressed in white, one tall and the other smaller, were coolly debating as to whether the compartments would hold the ship afloat. They were standing with their backs to the rail looking on at the rest of the crew, and I recall asking one of them why he did not assist.

At this time there were other passengers around, but Clinch Smith was the only one associated with me here to the last. It was about this time, fifteen minutes after the launching of the last lifeboat on the port side, that I heard a noise that spread consternation among us all. This was no less than the water striking the bridge and gurgling up the hatchway forward. It seemed momentarily as if it would reach the Boat Deck. It appeared as if it would take the crew a long time to turn the Engelhardt boat right side up and lift it over the rail, and there were so many ready to board her that she would have been swamped. Probably taking these points into consideration, Clinch Smith made the proposition that we should leave and go toward the stern, still on the starboard side, so he started and I followed immediately after him. We had taken but a few steps in the direction indicated when there arose before us from the decks below, a mass of humanity several lines deep, covering the Boat Deck, facing us, and completely blocking our passage toward the stern.

There were women in the crowd, as well as men, and they seemed to be steerage passengers who had just come up from the decks below. Instantly, when they saw us and the water on the deck chasing us from behind, they turned in the opposite direction towards the stern. This brought them at that point plumb against the iron fence and railing which divide the first and second cabin passengers. Even among these people there was no hysterical cry, or evidence of panic, but oh, the agony of it! Clinch Smith and I instantly saw that we could make no progress ahead, and with the water following us behind over the deck, we were in a desperate place. I can never forget the exact point on the ship where he and I were located, viz., at the opening of the angle made by the walls of the officers' house and only a short distance abaft the *Titanic's* forward "expansion joint." Clinch Smith was immediately on my left, nearer the apex of the angle, and our backs were turned toward the ship's rail and the sea. Looking up toward the roof of the officers' house I saw a man to the right of me and above lying on his stomach on the roof, with his legs dangling over. Clinch Smith jumped to reach this roof, and I promptly followed. The efforts of both of us failed. I was loaded down with heavy long-skirted overcoat and Norfolk coat beneath, with clumsy life-preserver over all, which made my jump fall short. As I came down, the water struck my right side. I crouched down into it preparatory to jumping with it, and rose as if on the crest of a wave on the seashore. This expedient brought the attainment of the object I had in view. I was able to reach the roof and the iron railing that is along the edge of it, and pulled myself over on top of the officers' house on my stomach near the base of the second funnel. The feat which I instinctively accomplished was the simple one, familiar to all bathers in the surf at the seashore. I had no time to advise Clinch Smith to adopt it. To my utter dismay, a hasty glance to my left and right showed that he had not followed my example, and that the wave, if I may call it such, which had mounted me to the roof, had completely covered him, as well as all people on both sides of me, including the man I had first seen athwart the roof.

I was thus parted forever from my friend, Clinch Smith, with whom I had agreed to remain to the last struggle. I felt almost a pang of responsibility for our separation; but he was not in sight and there was no chance of rendering assistance. His ultimate fate is a matter of conjecture. Hemmed in by the mass of people toward the stern, and cornered in the locality previously described, it seems certain that as the ship keeled over and sank, his body was caught in the angle or in the coils of rope and other appurtenances on the deck and born down to the depths below. There could not be a braver man than James Clinch Smith. He was the embodiment of coolness and courage during the whole period of the disaster. While in constant touch and communication with him at the various points on the ship when we were together on this tragic night, he never showed the slightest sign of fear, but manifested the same quiet imperturbable manner so well known to all of his friends, who join with his family in mourning his loss. His conduct should be an inspiration to us all, and an appropriate epitaph to his memory taken from the words of Christ would be: "Greater love hath no man than this, that a man lay down his life for his friend."

The peculiar way in which the *Titanic* is described as hesitating and assuming a vertical position before her final dive to the depths below can be accounted for only on the hypothesis of the sliding of the boilers from their beds. A second cabin passenger, Mr Lawrence Beesley, a Cambridge University man, has written an excellent book about the *Titanic* disaster, dwelling especially upon the lessons to be learned from it. His account given to the newspapers also contains the most graphic description from the viewpoint of those in the lifeboats, telling how the great ship looked before her final plunge. He "was a mile or two miles away," he writes, "when the oarsmen lay on their oars and all in the lifeboat were motionless as we watched the ship in absolute silence – save some who would not look and buried their heads on each others' shoulders. . . . As we gazed awe-struck, she tilted slightly up, revolving apparently about a centre of gravity just astern of amidships until she attained a vertical upright position, and there she remained – motionless! As she swung up, her lights, which had shown without a flicker all night, went out suddenly, then came on again for a

single flash and then went out altogether; and as they did so there came a noise which many people, wrongly, I think, have described as an explosion. It has always seemed to me that it was nothing but the engines and machinery coming loose from their place and bearings and falling through the compartments, smashing everything in their way. It was partly a roar, partly a groan, partly a rattle and partly a smash, and it was not a sudden roar as an explosion would be; it went on successively for some seconds, possibly fifteen or twenty, as the heavy machinery dropped down to the bottom (now the bows) of the ship; I suppose it fell through the end and sank first before the ship. But it was a noise no one had heard before and no one wishes to hear again. It was stupefying, stupendous, as it came to us along the water. It was as if all the heavy things one could think of had been thrown downstairs from the top of a house, smashing each other, and the stairs and everything in the way. . ."

. . .But let me now resume my personal narrative. With this second wind under water there came to me a new lease of life and strength, until finally I noticed by the increase of light that I was drawing near to the surface. Though it was not daylight, the clear star-lit night made a noticeable difference in the degree of light immediately below the surface of the water. As I was rising, I came in contact with ascending wreckage, but the only thing I struck of material size was a small plank, which I tucked under my right arm. This circumstance brought with it the reflection that it was advisable for me to secure what best I could to keep me afloat on the surface until succour arrived. When my head at last rose above the water, I detected a piece of wreckage like a wooden crate, and I eagerly seized it as a nucleus of the projected raft to be constructed from what flotsam and jetsam I might collect. Looking about me, I could see no *Titanic* in sight. She had entirely disappeared beneath the calm surface of the ocean and without a sign of any wave. That the sea had swallowed her up with all her precious belongings was indicated by the slight sound of a gulp behind me as the water closed over her. The length of time that I was under water can be estimated by the fact that I sank with her, and when I came up there was no ship in sight. The accounts of others as to the length of time it took the *Titanic* to sink afford the best measure of the interval I was below the surface.

What impressed me at the time that my eyes beheld the horrible scene was a thin light-grey smoky vapour that hung like a pall a few feet above the broad expanse of sea that was covered with a mass of tangled wreckage. That it was a tangible vapour, and not a product of imagination, I feel well assured. It may have been caused by smoke or steam rising to the surface around the area where the ship had sunk. At any rate it produced a supernatural effect, and the pictures I had seen by Dante and the description I had read in my Virgil of the infernal regions, of Charon, and the River Lethe, were then uppermost in my thoughts. Add to this, within the area described, which was as far as my eyes could reach, there arose to the sky the most horrible sounds ever heard by mortal man except by those of us who survived this terrible tragedy. The agonizing cries of death from over a thousand throats, the wails and groans of the suffering, the shrieks of the terror-stricken and the awful gaspings for breath of those in the last throes of drowning, none of us will ever forget to our dying day. "Help! Help! Boat ahoy! Boat ahoy!" and "My God! My God!" were the heart-rending cries and shrieks of men, which floated to us over the surface of the dark waters continuously for the next hour, but as time went on, growing weaker and weaker until they died out entirely.

As I clung to my wreckage, I noticed just in front of me, a few yards away, a group of three bodies with heads in the water, face downwards, and just behind me to my right another body, all giving unmistakable evidence of

being drowned. Possibly these had gone down to the depths as I had done, but did not have the lung power that I had to hold the breath and swim under water, an accomplishment which I had practised from my school days. There was no one alive or struggling in the water or calling for aid within the immediate vicinity of where I arose to the surface. I threw my right leg over the wooden crate in an attempt to straddle and balance myself on top of it, but I turned over in a somersault with it under water, and up to the surface again.

I espied to my left, a considerable distance away, a better vehicle of escape than the wooden crate on which my attempt to ride had resulted in a second ducking. What I saw was no less than the same Engelhardt, or "surf-boat", to whose launching I had lent my efforts, until the water broke upon the ship's Boat Deck where we were. On top of this upturned boat, half reclining on her bottom, were now more than a dozen men, whom, by their dress, I took to be all members of the crew of the ship. Thank God, I did not hesitate a moment in discarding the friendly crate that had been my first aid. I struck out through the wreckage and after a considerable swim reached the port side amidships of this Engelhardt boat, which with her companions, wherever utilized, did good service in saving the lives of many others.

When I reached the side of the boat I met with a doubtful reception, and, as no extending hand was held out to me, I grabbed, by the muscle of the left arm, a young member of the crew nearest and facing me. At the same time I threw my right leg over the boat astraddle, pulling myself aboard,with a friendly lift to my foot given by someone astern as I assumed a reclining position with them on the bottom of the capsized boat. Then after me came a dozen other swimmers who clambered around and whom we helped aboard. Among them was one completely exhausted, who came on the same port side as myself. I pulled him in and he lay face downward in front of me for several hours, until just before dawn he was able to stand up with the rest of us. The moment of getting aboard this upturned boat was one of supreme mental relief, more so than any other until I reached the deck of the hospitable *Carpathia* on the next morning.

THE SMALL WOMAN

ALAN BURGESS

Gladys Aylward, a former London parlour-maid, left for China in October 1930 with the determined ambition of becoming a missionary. After many appalling experiences with Japanese soldiers, she took a hundred homeless children over the mountains and across the Yellow River to Sian to protect them from the advancing Japanese army.

A T SUN-UP THE YOUNG CHILDREN were up and shouting, running round the courtyard, throwing their bundles of bedding at each other, playing "Tag" and generally behaving in the normal way of young children all over the world. With the aid of the older ones, Gladys tried to sort them out and feed them. There were nearly twenty big girls, ages varying from thirteen to fifteen, Ninepence and Sualan amongst them: there were seven big boys aged between eleven and fifteen; the rest of the children varied from four to eight, wild, undisciplined, laughing, weeping, shouting little brats. In vain, she tried to tell them that they must save their energy for the long day ahead; she might just as usefully have told a stream to stop running. The two coolies from the Mandarin, carrying their shoulder-poles, a basket of millet suspended at either end, arrived at the front gate. Gladys said good-bye to the two Mission workers, to several other friends collected there; and, after one last look round the broken Inn, they were on their way, the children scampering ahead, dodging back through the gates of the city, shouting loudly that they could walk for ever and ever.

They followed the main trail southwards for several miles. Gladys possessed a whistle which she had obtained from a Japanese soldier months before, and she blew it occasionally to call the more adventurous little boys down from outcrops of rock, and twice to line them all up in rows for a roll-call to see that no one was missing.

They stopped by a stream to boil millet in the iron pot which Gladys carried; she heaped the steaming grain into the basins as each child came up in turn for its helping. At the end of this serving there wasn't much left in the pot for her, and from that moment onwards that was the way things usually turned out. The children, revived after the meal, began to clamber about the rocks again, and made excited forays ahead, to lie in wait and ambush the main party. She gave up trying to keep them in order, but as the afternoon progressed, these minor expeditions became fewer and fewer, and soon she had four small ones hanging on to her coat, protesting that they were tired, and could they all go back to Yangcheng now? Gladys took it in turns with the older boys to carry them. She felt a little tired herself.

It was getting dark when they came to a mountain village she knew, and where she thought they might find shelter for the night. Not, she thought, that any householders would be particularly anxious to house a hundred noisy, dirty children. Help came from an unexpected quarter. An old Buddhist priest, in his bright saffron robes, stood on the steps of his temple as the Pied Piper of Yangcheng and her brood straggled past.

"Where are you going?" he called to Gladys.

"We are refugees on the way to Sian," she said.

He came down the steps and approached her, his small eyes almost lost in the maze of wrinkles and lines that creased his face.

"But what are you going to do with all these children, woman?" He sounded most disapproving.

"I'm looking for a place for us to sleep tonight."

"Then you can stay in the temple," he said abruptly. "All my brother priests are away. There is plenty of room. Tell them to come in. It will be warmer than the mountainside."

The children needed no prompting. This was something like an adventure! It was dark in the temple, and there were gloomy recesses in which stone figures of the fat, bland, heavy-lidded Buddha resided. There were painted panels depicting the many tortures of sinners, but the children were too tired to notice them. They crowded round the iron pot when Gladys had finished cooking the millet, and when they had eaten, they curled up on their bedding and went fast asleep.

She did not sleep so easily. For one thing, the temple was alive with rats, who twittered in the darkness and ran over the sleeping children; and a small creeping doubt had

entered her mind concerning the wisdom of starting this
journey with so many small ones. Perhaps she was over-
estimating her own ability? It was one thing to journey
through the mountains alone; quite another to take a
hundred children with you. The first day had been
troublesome enough, yet all the children were fresh, and
she was crossing country she knew intimately. The older
girls had not complained, but she could see that several of
them had suffered already. They were completely unused
to mountain walking; the feet of several of them had once
been bound, and even many years free from the bindings
was insufficient to turn them into healthy limbs able to
withstand the drag and scrape of the rocky paths. For
perhaps an hour the big boys tried to keep off the rats,
then they also became too tired to persevere and fell
asleep. Gladys lay on the hard floor; above her head the
impassive sculptured face of the stone Buddha was
illumined by a shaft of moonlight streaming downwards
through some aperture high above. The more she thought

about the future, the less she liked it, but there was no chance of retreat now; she had to go on.

The next day was a replica of the first. The children awoke refreshed, and with a complete lack of reverence began to explore the temple with shrill, admiring cries. The priest smiled urbanely; he did not seem to mind at all. He bowed when Gladys offered her thanks and wished her a safe journey to Sian.

They were far from any village when the next night caught them, and they huddled together in the shelter of a semi-circle of rocks out of the wind. In the night there was a heavy mist and the children crept under their wet quilts, and next day they steamed and dried out when the sun rose. That afternoon they met a man on a mule travelling in the same direction as themselves. If they would come to his village, he said, he would be glad to find them shelter for the night. She accepted his offer gratefully. In his courtyard the children spread themselves out and scooped cooked millet out of their bowls until their bellies were full, then drank cupful after cupful of the hot twig tea. They still thought it was all a wonderful adventure. Even Gladys felt an immense sense of relief with another day safely past, and the Yellow River one day closer. She cupped her bowl between her hands, embracing the tiny warmth it offered, and chatted to the other girls.

"How many days will it take us to reach the Yellow River, Ai-weh-deh?" asked Sualan diffidently.

Although Gladys had never been through to the Yellow River, she knew the answer to that question without any trouble. "The muleteers on the normal track used to take five days. We're going right through the mountains. About twelve, I'd say."

"And we shan't see a single Japanese soldier the whole way?" asked Ninepence.

"I hope not," she answered.

She looked at the two girls as they chatted, the girl she had bought for ninepence, and the slave girl from the *yamen.* They were both exquisite little creatures with clear pale skins and blue-black shining hair. Even in their dusty padded coats their prettiness was still unimpaired. She thought wistfully how beautiful they would look in the ceremonial robes of China, wondering if they would ever know such luxury. How absurd that they should be forced to make this long journey to save their lives. She felt an unreasoning anger at the stupidity of all men that they should be the cause of this ordeal. She yawned. It was odd, this constant tiredness. "Probably the added responsibility of the children," she thought to herself, as she wrapped herself in her bedding quilt and lay down to sleep.

In the morning the two carriers of the millet had to return to Yangcheng. They had reached the limit of their province. However, the man they had met in the mountains proved a good friend; he provided them with another coolie who would carry what was left of the millet until it was finished, and even by rationing it did not look as if that would last another two days.

The next two nights were spent in the open. Two of the older boys, Teh and Liang, had obtained a pot of whitewash from a village along the way, and they went on ahead daubing a splash of white on to the rocks to mark the trail across the mountains. Sometimes they would write a text across a rock: "This is the way. Walk ye in it!" or "Fear ye not, little flock!" There were squeals of appreciation as the messages were translated to the young ones.

This was new country to Gladys, but she knew they were heading south by the direction of the sun. They were thirsty practically all the time, for the sun was hot and wells were only to be found in the villages. After the heavy wet mountain mists each morning they would gather round any drip from the rocks and moisten their tongues. The millet was used up now, and the carrier went back to his village. They had no more food, and the

mountains stretched ahead of them, wild and barren, with few places of habitation. Often, when they climbed over virgin rock, the slopes were so steep that they had to form a human chain down the mountain-side, and pass the younger children down from hand to hand. They cried when they fell down, and cried when they got tired. Often Gladys tried to rally them with a hymn, and when they reached a level patch of ground they would all march bravely along singing the chorus. Between them, the older children and Gladys were carrying practically all the bedding now, and often they would give one of the five or six-year-olds a pick-a-back ride for a short distance. There was rarely any moment when a small hand was not clutching at Gladys's jacket.

Seven nights out from Yangcheng found them camped in the heart of a mountainous region unknown to her. They had found a small trail which led southwards. It was not yet dark, but everyone was too exhausted to move farther. The thin, home-made cloth shoes, which everyone wore, were practically all worn out. The big girls' feet were cut and bleeding. Everyone was filthy, covered with dust and dirt; they had no food. Gladys raised her head to scan the party lying in huddled groups under the rocks. She did not like what she saw; unless they received food and help very soon, she was afraid of what might happen to them. Suddenly she saw Teh and Liang, who were still acting as forward scouts, running back towards her. They were shouting something which she could not hear, but their obvious excitement presaged danger.

"Men!" they shouted. "Soldiers!"

Gladys froze in a moment of panic. She put her whistle into her mouth to blow the pre-arranged signal for the children to scatter, but she did not blow it. If they scattered into this wild terrain they might all be lost and would starve or die in the wilderness. And then, as the boys stumbled towards her, she saw men in uniform rounding a buttress of rock down the valley, and with a gasping sigh of relief realised that they were Nationalist troops. The children had sighted them also. Their tiredness fell away and they bounded over the rocks to greet the newcomers. Gladys, with the girls, advanced more slowly, and as she walked suddenly heard the sound she dreaded more than any other. The noise of aircraft engines! With a thunder of sound that echoed throughout the valley, two Japanese fighters tore through a cleft in the mountains and hurtled across their heads. Although they must have been hundreds of feet up, their sudden appearance, the abrupt bull-roar of their engines sent a shock-wave of panic through everyone in the valley.

She threw herself into the shelter of a rock, glimpsing from the corner of her eye that the girls were doing the same. She crouched, rigid, waiting for the rattle of machine-guns. None came. She looked up, as the planes disappeared, catching sight of the stubby wings, the "Rising Sun" insignia painted on the fuselage. But the airmen were obviously intent on something more important than machine-gunning Nationalist troops or refugees in the mountains. Gladys stood up and looked down the valley. The children had been well trained on their drill in the event of attack by aircraft. They were scrambling up from their hiding-places. The Nationalist troops, who had also scattered wildly, were mixed up with the children. They rose from the rocks, laughing together.

There were about fifty soldiers, reinforcements from Honan passing up country to join a Nationalist force farther north. Gladys met the young officer in charge, and explained their predicament, but the problem of the hungry children was being solved spontaneously. Soldiers were diving their hands into knapsacks, and bringing out treasures of sweet foods, and all round she could hear only the "Ahs!" and "Oohs!" and "Ohs!" of the delighted children.

The soldiers decided to camp in that spot for the night. They invited Gladys and her brood to stay with them and share their food. It was a feast! They had foodstuffs not seen in Shansi for years. The children sat round the small fires, stuffing themselves to bursting point. Even Gladys, for the first time on the journey, ate her fill. When the troops moved on at dawn the children waved them a sorrowful good-bye.

THE LETTER "A"

CHRISTY BROWN

from My Left Foot

Christy Brown (1932-1981) was born with severe cerebral palsy but his almost helpless body concealed a brilliant and imaginative mind. He managed to overcome his physical disability with the help of his family and his doctor, and published a novel about life in Dublin, called Down All the Days, *which became an immediate best-seller. He wrote a number of other successful books, including an autobiography,* My Left Foot.

A T THIS TIME my mother had the five other children to look after besides the "difficult one", though as yet it was not by any means a full house. There were my brothers, Jim, Tony and Paddy, and my two sisters, Lily and Mona, all of them very young, just a year or so between each of them, so that they were almost exactly like steps of stairs.

Four years rolled by and I was now five, and still as helpless as a newly-born baby. While my father was out at bricklaying earning our bread and butter for us, mother was slowly, patiently pulling down the wall, brick by brick, that seemed to thrust itself between me and the other children, slowly, patiently penetrating beyond the thick curtain that hung over my mind, separating it from theirs. It was hard, heart-breaking work, for often all she got from me in return was a vague smile and perhaps a faint gurgle. I could not speak or even mumble, nor could I sit up without support on my own, let alone take steps. But I wasn't inert or motionless. I seemed indeed to be convulsed with movement, wild, stiff, snake-like movement that never left me, except in sleep. My fingers twisted and twitched continually, my arms twined backwards and would often shoot out suddenly this way and that, and my head lolled and sagged sideways. I was a queer, crooked little fellow.

Mother tells me how one day she had been sitting with me for hours in an upstairs room, showing me pictures out of a great big storybook that I had got from Santa Claus last Christmas and telling me the names of the different animals and flowers that were in them, trying without success to get me to repeat them. This had gone on for hours while she talked and laughed with me. Then at the end of it she leaned over me and said gently into my ear:

"Did you like it, Chris? Did you like the bears and the monkeys and all the lovely flowers? Nod your head for yes, like a good boy."

But I could make no sign that I had understood her. Her face was bent over mine, hopefully. Suddenly, involuntarily, my queer hand reached up and grasped one of the dark curls that fell in a thick cluster about her neck. Gently she loosened the clenched fingers, though some dark strands were still clutched between them.

Then she turned away from my curious stare and left the room, crying. The door closed behind her. It all seemed hopeless. It looked as though there was some justification for my relatives' contention that I was an idiot and beyond help.

They now spoke of an institution.

"Never!" said my mother almost fiercely, when this was suggested to her. "I know my boy is not an idiot. It is his body that is shattered, not his mind. I'm sure of that."

Sure? Yet inwardly, she prayed God would give her some proof of her faith. She knew it was one thing to believe but quite another thing to prove.

I was now five, and still I showed no real sign of intelligence. I showed no apparent interest in things except with my toes – more especially those of my left foot. Although my natural habits were clean I could not aid myself, but in this respect my father took care of me. I used to lie on my back all the time in the kitchen or, on bright warm days, out in the garden, a little bundle of crooked muscles and twisted nerves, surrounded by a family that loved me and hoped for me and that made me part of their own warmth and humanity. I was lonely, imprisoned in a world of my own, unable to communicate with others, cut off, separated from them as though a glass wall stood between my existence and theirs, thrusting me beyond the sphere of their lives and activities. I longed to run about and play with the rest, but I was unable to break loose from my bondage.

Then, suddenly, it happened! In a moment everything was changed, my future life moulded into a definite shape, my mother's faith in me rewarded and her secret fear changed into open triumph.

It happened so quickly, so simply after all the years of waiting and uncertainty that I can see and feel the whole scene as if it had happened last week. It was the afternoon of a cold, grey December day. The streets outside glistened with snow; the white sparkling flakes stuck and melted on the window-panes and hung on the boughs of the trees like molten silver. The wind howled dismally, whipping up little whirling columns of snow that rose and fell at every fresh gust. And over all, the dull, murky sky stretched like a dark canopy, a vast infinity of greyness.

Inside, all the family were gathered round the big kitchen fire that lit up the little room with a warm glow and made giant shadows dance on the walls and ceiling.

In a corner Mona and Paddy were sitting huddled together, a few torn school primers before them. They were writing down little sums on to an old chipped slate,

using a bright piece of yellow chalk. I was close to them, propped up by a few pillows against the wall, watching.

It was the chalk that attracted me so much. It was a long slender stick of vivid yellow. I had never seen anything like it before, and it showed up so well against the black surface of the slate that I was fascinated by it as much as if it had been a stick of gold.

Suddenly I wanted desperately to do what my sister was doing. Then – without thinking or knowing exactly what I was doing, I reached out and took the stick of chalk out of my sister's hand – *with my left foot*.

I do not know why I used my left foot to do this. It is a puzzle to many people as well as to myself, for, although I had displayed a curious interest in my toes at an early age, I had never attempted before this to use either of my feet in any way. They could have been as useless to me as were my hands. That day, however, my left foot, apparently on its own volition, reached out and very impolitely took the chalk out of my sister's hand.

I held it tightly between my toes, and, acting on an impulse, made a wild sort of scribble with it on the slate. Next moment I stopped, a bit dazed, surprised, looking down at the stick of yellow chalk stuck between my toes, not knowing what to do with it next, hardly knowing how it got there. Then I looked up and became aware that everyone had stopped talking and were staring at me silently. Nobody stirred. Mona, her black curls framing her chubby little face, stared at me with great big eyes and open mouth. Across the open hearth, his face lit by flames, sat my father, leaning forward, hands outspread on his knees, his shoulders tense. I felt the sweat break out on my forehead.

My mother came in from the pantry with a steaming pot in her hand. She stopped midway between the table and the fire, feeling the tension flowing through the room. She followed their stare and saw me, in the corner. Her eyes looked from my face down to my foot, with the chalk gripped between my toes. She put down the pot.

Then she crossed over to me and knelt down beside me, as she had done so many times before.

"I'll show you what do to with it, Chris," she said, very slowly and in a queer, jerky way, her face flushed as if with some inner excitement.

Taking another piece of chalk from Mona, she hesitated, then very deliberately drew, on the floor in front of me, *the single letter "A"*.

"Copy that," she said, looking steadily at me. "Copy it, Christy."

I couldn't.

I looked about me, looked around at the faces that were turned towards me, tense, excited faces that were at that moment frozen, immobile, eager, waiting for a miracle in their midst.

The stillness was profound. The room was full of flame and shadow that danced before my eyes and lulled my taut nerves into a sort of waking sleep. I could hear the sound of the water-tap dripping in the pantry, the loud ticking of the clock on the mantelshelf, and the soft hiss and crackle of the logs on the open hearth.

I tried again. I put out my foot and made a wild jerking stab with the chalk which produced a very crooked line and nothing more. Mother held the slate steady for me.

"Try again, Chris," she whispered in my ear. "Again."

I did. I stiffened my body and put my left foot out again, for the third time. I drew one side of the letter. I drew half the other side. Then the stick of chalk broke and I was left with a stump. I wanted to fling it away and give up. Then I felt my mother's hand on my shoulder. I tried once more. Out went my foot. I shook, I sweated and strained every muscle. My hands were so tightly clenched that my fingernails bit into the flesh. I set my teeth so hard that I nearly pierced my lower lip. Everything in the room swam

till the faces around me were mere patches of white. But –
I drew it – *the letter "A"*. There it was on the floor before
me. Shaky, with awkward, wobbly sides and a very
uneven centre line. But it *was* the letter "A". I looked up. I
saw my mother's face for a moment, tears on her cheeks.
Then my father stooped down and hoisted me on to his
shoulder.

I had done it! It had started – the thing that was to give
my mind its chance of expressing itself. True, I couldn't
speak with my lips, but now I would speak through
something more lasting than spoken words – written
words.

That one letter, scrawled on the floor with a broken bit
of yellow chalk gripped between my toes, was my road to
a new world, my key to mental freedom. It was to provide
a source of relaxation to the tense, taut thing that was me
which panted for expression behind a twisted mouth.

THE STRUGGLE IS MY LIFE

S. R. 'MAC' MAHARAJ

S.R. 'Mac' Maharaj was sentenced to twelve years imprisonment on South Africa's notorious Robben Island in December 1964. Among his fellow prisoners was Nelson Mandela. Whilst in hiding from the authorities in June 1961, Mandela wrote, "The struggle is my life. I will continue fighting for freedom until the end of my days." Three years later he was sentenced to life imprisonment on Robben Island and was later kept under close house arrest until his release in 1990. In 1994 Nelson Mandela was elected President of South Africa. In this extract from an interview conducted in London in 1978 by a member of the Research, Information and Publications Department of the International Defence and Aid Fund for Southern Africa, Maharaj talks about the kind of prison conditions he shared with Mandela.

Q *WHAT KIND OF CELL does Mandela have?*
A. He has been living in a concrete cell, outside walls of grey stone 7 ft by 7 ft and about 9 ft high. It was lit with one 40 watt globe. It had originally no furnishings except for a bed roll and mat, no bench, no table, nothing. Then as a result of demands made by us some were provided with small tables 2 ft by 2 ft 6 in and later on it was extended to all the prisoners in that section and they built post office type counters against the wall without benches, you had to stand and work. They then provided benches and one wooden shelf, just a plank to keep your books on but we ourselves got cardboard paper

and plastic and made cupboards for ourselves. Somewhere around 1973-74 when Nelson was ill he was granted a bed for the first time, so in his cell there is a bed. Then I think, oh yes, as a result of his back trouble he received a chair instead of a bench.

Q. *Does he have hot water to wash in?*

A. From the beginning of our imprisonment up to 1973 we only had access to cold water. There were periods when they changed the water for bathing to sea water instead of brack water. They reverted to brack water for washing and provided fresh water brought from the mainland in drums for us to drink from. They introduced hot water into the isolation section in 1973 – a little earlier in the main sections of the prison. There are communal showers. Now again, typically of the administration, you will find that these facilities which you begin to enjoy are then used as forms of punishment. It is difficult to talk of hot water for showering without remembering that in mid-winter we will find that when we are engaged in some struggle against the authorities, suddenly there is no hot water and that will go on for weeks and weeks. The same thing will happen with the taped music they were playing for us. Once you've got used to it the next thing it is used as a form of punishment – it is taken away. Of course they do not say it is a form of punishment but you will find that it's out of order for six months or a year.

Q. *What toilet facilities are available?*

A. In the single cell section we have communal toilets to which we have no access except when the cells are opened. In your cells when you are confined – and you spend an average of 15 hours on weekdays, and during weekends up to 17 hours or more in your cell – you are provided with a sanitary pail, and you are given a plastic bottle which takes about $1^1/_2$ pints of water for drinking purposes or any other use while you are locked up.

Q. *What diet does Mandela have? How does it compare with that of other prisoners?*

A. Right at the beginning of his imprisonment and when Nelson got to Robben Island as part of the Rivonia group he was offered by the head of prison security a special diet. Nelson refused because he realised that it was a subterfuge based not on his actual medical condition but merely a roundabout way of giving him a diet different from his colleagues. So his diet has been the normal prisoners' diet which of course discriminates on the basis of whether you are African, Coloured, or Indian. Just to illustrate how it works: there is porridge for breakfast (maize-meal porridge) for all – but African comrades are allowed half a tablespoon of sugar – Indians and Coloureds one tablespoon. At lunchtime Africans may be given plain boiled mealies and perhaps boiled samp the next day, both being different forms of maize. Now Indians and Coloureds in the same section might also get samp but not on the day when the African comrades get it, and then the next day might get mealie rice which is just more crushed maize. So that although you have to eat food which is classified differently according to race, in fact it is mostly different forms of the same thing – maize. Now Nelson is treated in the same way with the difference that in recent years his meal has been salt-free.

In 1973-74 when he was not well – the result of high blood pressure – he was given treatment, a bed and he was put on a supplementary medical diet. He also has to have a salt-free diet so that his food comes separately. It's the same food but it's prepared without salt and in addition he has been given milk.

Q. *How are prisoners separated from each other and how many groups are there?*

A. When I was on the island there were three groups of prisoners – those in the "single cells", which included the prisoners from the Rivonia trial and others and Toivo of SWAPO. Then there are the main sections which are communal cells divided into two sections with a wall separating them. One houses primarily the South African political prisoners but includes some short-term Namibian prisoners. Then there is the other communal section, a smaller section housing primarily the Namibian comrades, but it includes some South Africans sentenced under the Terrorism Act including quite a few ANC men.

Since March 1977 another communal section has been built where they now hold the people sentenced in the last two years, particularly the younger ones, in an attempt to keep them isolated from the bulk of the prisoners.

We don't know how they categorised us – I don't know why they put me in the single cells, for instance.

Q. *The thirty or so of you in the special section – were you all in single cells?*

A. All of us. This is the particular characteristic of the section that it is single cells, a cell for each person and you all have the same conditions.

Q. *Mandela is now an "A" Group prisoner. What does this mean in terms of letters and visits?*

A. Well, he is allowed three outgoing and three incoming letters a month. He is allowed two visits of two people at a time for half an hour per visit per month.

According to regulations "A" group prisoners should be allowed "contact" visits, but political prisoners are not allowed these. Also, "A" group prisoners should be allowed access to newspapers and radio broadcasts, which again they are not allowed.

Q. *What work has Mandela done on the island? What is he doing now?*

A. When Nelson was sentenced in 1962 he was kept in Pretoria Central jail in solitary confinement. He was then shifted to Robben Island in 1963 – he stayed two weeks on Robben Island without work, confined to his cell. Suddenly he was taken back to Pretoria into solitary and then brought to trial in the Rivonia case. He was sentenced in June 1964, taken with his comrades to Robben Island, kept in a zinc section (a temporary section) in total isolation and solitary confinement and then brought to the present single cells which were specially built for the Rivonia men. There they were first kept in total isolation.

They were then put to breaking stones in the yard with a four-pound hammer, crushing them to little pieces. This is where I joined them and we did that job until February 1965 when we were taken to the lime quarry, which meant digging limestone with a pick and shovel, cutting it and loading it on to trucks. This work was our main form of activity right until 1973-74. It was interspersed with very short bouts of other work – at one time building a road to the airport of Robben Island and at other times repairing the surface of the hardground road. In 1973-74 we were taken for the first time to the sea where we collected seaweed with our bare hands. This was alternate work, we sometimes did seaweed work, sometimes the lime work. The lime work was one the authorities had promised the

Red Cross they would stop and despite their promises they only stopped it somewhere around 1975.

The latest report I have is that since I left the island at the beginning of November 1976 the comrades in the single cells have not been out to work at all and have therefore spent virtually a year and a half in total inactivity. This is at a time when their studies have been curtailed, which means that most of those in the single cells are not studying. They are therefore confined once more, as we were when we were breaking stones, to the little quadrangle which is slightly larger than a tennis court and they therefore have no chance of even seeing a blade of grass except when they go out to receive visits.

Q. *Tell us about this quadrangle?*

A. It's supposed to be an exercise yard and in about 1975 they allowed us to construct a volleyball court in it. We constructed it ourselves and adjusted it into a sort of tennis court – but with 30 prisoners you must appreciate

you can't all play tennis and not all of them are fit enough to play tennis. In fact, I have one comrade who says that a present they are not working and it is completely monotonous, he says weekends have lost their meaning; every day is just the same. And of course, we have repeatedly demanded creative work: pottery, carpentry, basket-making, where you work at your own speed and you do something creative and can see what you are producing. But the authorities have been adamant in refusing this kind of work.

Q. *What is a routine day for Mandela on the island? Could you give a brief summary of a day for the single cell prisoners?*

A. I'll give a typical day of the last two years of my prison life, that is between 1974 and 1976.

You are woken up at different times in winter or summer, earlier in summer, later in winter. Summer at five, winter about six. When you are woken up you go out through the corridor into a section where there are communal baths and toilets. You are allowed about half an hour for everyone to wash and to clean their sanitary pails. There are about four sinks where all 30 may wash and shave. It is mandatory that you shave, as well as clean your sanitary pail. If you want to have a bath you must have it within that half an hour.

Then you collect your food. The food is brought in drums into the section, left at the gate where it is collected and we then dish it out ourselves, organising ourselves into teams voluntarily to do this work. You have your breakfast and within an hour from opening the doors you are supposed to fall in, unless of course the warders are late. You then go out to work. There were times in the early years when we were allowed the luxury of walking to our workplace, which enabled us to see something of the island, but then they began to move us by truck to prevent us from coming across any other prisoners. You get to work and you go down to work, say clearing seaweed, and you go on doing this until lunchbreak, which is an hour's break. The food is brought in drums, we dish it out and we sit down on the ground – open air, no tables – for eating utensils we are provided with a spoon and a steel plate. You knock off work at any time between half past three and four, the timing being determined by the fact that you must be back in the prison and given about half an hour for all the prisoners to have a bath and the food to be dished out and cleared by the prisoners. Then you are locked up by half past four or quarter to five so that the warders can sign off by five and the next shift of warders can come on. And from five if you are not allowed study privilege you are allowed to be up and about in your cell until eight o'clock when you are supposed to be in bed. Those who are allowed to study at the level of matriculation (which is roughly the equivalent of GCSE) are allowed until ten o'clock at night to study; those who are allowed university status could go on until eleven. When you are supposed to go to sleep the lights

remain on and you are meant to be in bed, not even reading. If a warder finds you reading after those hours he can have you charged and punished for it. In the early 1970s they introduced a canned music service. This music was played from lock-up or from about six to eight pm. Neither at Christmas, New Year or any other occasion are you allowed to sing or whistle, either individually or communally. That is the typical day.

CHILDREN OF THE SIEGE

PAULINE CUTTING

Having only recently qualified as a surgeon, Doctor Pauline Cutting volunteered to go to Beirut in 1985, during the civil war, to work in a badly damaged hospital constantly under attack by the Amal militia. She considered that her skills in burns treatment and plastic surgery would be of use. Later, she moved to Bourj al Barajneh, a Palestinian refugee camp which was under siege.

O N SATURDAY, MAY 31, I woke up with jolt at 5 a.m. It was still dark. Bombs were exploding all around every few seconds. A deafening crash thundered above me, delivering a whack in the chest, like a body blow, as the shock wave hit the hospital. The whole building shuddered and I could hear the sounds of smashing glass, of bricks and rubble falling. "O God," I thought, "the whole hospital is falling down!" I scrambled out of bed and dashed out into the corridor with Lieve and Dirk. A large shell had made a direct hit on the hospital. It was followed closely by a second and a third.

People came crowding into the corridor from their rooms. Children were crying. Nurses were helping those who could walk down the stairs from the first floor above us. Up there people were screaming.

Khaled, a young hospital administrator, whose main occupation, I thought, was maintaining the crease in his immaculately pressed trousers and smiling and joking with girls, charged blindly up the stairs into the billowing dust and smoke. He pushed between a nurse and an old man recovering from pneumonia, severing the drip connection, and with other young men close behind him, began rescuing bedridden patients, carrying them down the stairs in their beds, as bombs shook the building every few seconds. It was an extraordinary demonstration of selfless courage.

A seriously wounded man, upstairs because our 'Intensive Care Unit' was full, was hurriedly put down in the corridor, chest tube, drips, bags and all, amongst the feet of the sheltering people. His colostomy bag had come adrift and I got down on my knees on the floor and tried to clean him up, set right all his tubes and make him comfortable.

Astonishingly, no one was injured in the hospital. A boy with a broken leg told me excitedly how a tank shell had come in through the window of his ward, shot past the feet of his and another boy's beds, gone out of the door, across the corridor, through another room housing an old lady, and buried itself in the far wall without exploding.

The blanket bombardment went on for three hours with bombs exploding everywhere in the camp every few seconds. The noise was deafening. Initially, I went downstairs towards the emergency room but Samir, the radiographer, guided me to the safety of a corridor behind the emergency room saying that the brick outside wall of the emergency room was not enough protection from these shells. We lived through the shelling out in the crowded corridor, dashing into the emergency room to attend to the wounded, then retiring again to the safety of the corridor.

Extraordinarily, there were only five or so casualties during that whole three hours and they all had only minor wounds. I think it was because the bombing started so early in the morning and most people were asleep in the shelters or in their homes. Once it started, it was suicidal to venture outside anywhere. But it was still amazing, as whole houses of flimsy breeze-blocks and plaster could be completely demolished by a direct hit in such an attack.

The ordeal of the bombardment was lightened by a constant supply of sweet black Arab tea. By now I had grown to like it very much and I found it calmed my nerves. The Arabs drink at least as much tea as the British, which was great for a tea addict like me. The right time for tea was all the time.

Of course we now knew that tanks were stationed around the camp. As the shelling went on, one of the male nurses explained the different types of bombs to me. Tank shells travel in virtually a straight line when they leave the the muzzle, so they hit the first obstacle in their path. Only the top floors of the hospital were exposed to these because the basement, ground floor and part of the first floor were shielded by surrounding houses. Rockets, which were the ones coming in threes and fours, were launched from the backs of trucks and fly in a slight arc. But the mortars fly up high and then drop, almost vertically, at the end of their flight, like the trajectory of a ball thrown over a high fence; these could drop into the narrow alleys and streets, exploding on impact. Bigger mortars could blow down walls but the smaller ones were only really dangerous to people caught outside.

Just after 8 a.m., the bombing died down and we drifted upstairs from the basement to the doctors' room, the room opposite mine. There was a brief breakfast and then we made our daily ward round. Abdul Feda was still complaining, "Oh, doctor, my arm hurts!" but now smiling with it. Fadi was doggedly optimistic as always, now with fewer tubes but still with a number yet to go. The others seemed to be speeding back to health. As so often I was amazed at the resilience of the human body.

We decided it was too dangerous to put patients back up on the first floor, so two other rooms on the ground floor next to mine were converted into wards and all the offices squeezed into one small one.

Once again our respite was brief. The bombing began again. A man was brought in dead, almost decapitated, and put straight into the fridge. Another had a high-velocity bullet injury of his thigh; the bullet had removed a large chunk of bone and severed the blood-vessels, so we operated to repair the vessels. Then a man was brought in with shrapnel in his chest. I took him to the room adjacent to the emergency room to put in a chest drain and was just preparing him on a low bed under the window when there was the flash and a huge bang just outside the window. Rubble and dust rained in on us. I dragged myself to my feet, checked that neither of us was wounded and calmly moved him to a bed away from the window. There had been no time to be frightened or to react in any way. It was all over before I understood what was happening and, because of that, was less frightening than I had imagined being very close to a bomb would be.

The bombing continued on and off for another week. The wards filled up and overflowed with patients. We opened up a room for them in the basement of the other wing of the hospital, but it was not well ventilated and a

long way from the emergency areas, so we tried to put only convalescent patients down there. There were not enough beds and three patients had to sleep on the large physiotherapy floor-mat which measured about two metres square. Despite the assistance of numerous volunteers who came to the hospital to do what they could to help us, the nurses were stretched to the limit.

We often had to drag the patients into the safety of the corridors, including two young men with broken thighs, who were confined completely to bed on home-made traction apparatus. They remained cheerful throughout. The heavier the bombardment, the more they laughed and joked, keeping people's spirits up. Once one of them called me over to look at his knees shaking in mock fear and I giggled. I found that a serious situation often produced incongruous results, and I often giggled during the shelling out of sheer nervousness. Dr Maher had a different reaction. He would go to sleep.

The two boys with fractured femurs spent several nights in the corridor, one behind the other against the wall, singing duets late into the night. An irascible old man in another bed sometimes lost his temper, shouting, "Shut up! Can no one be allowed to sleep around here?"

I now slept well despite all the noise, but bombing close by still woke me up. Lieve could sleep through anything, even a bomb landing on the hospital. One morning she wrote in her diary, "Quiet night, slept well," then looked at Dirk's diary, which said, "Heavy bombardment at 3 a.m."

Lieve, Dirk and I became very close during these weeks. We did not leave the confines of the hospital at all. In the evenings, whenever possible, we sat in our room to talk about patients and problems, or in the doctors' room where an old television was set up and we could watch the half-hour news in English at 6 p.m. and, incongruously, World Cup football from Mexico. Thair and his friend Ahmed came to visit us in our room, bringing us news from the front lines, which they said were holding steady.

On one side of the camp, the fighting was from building to building across a narrow street about ten metres wide, with the Palestinians and Amal shooting at each other from close range. When the fighting started, the houses on the edge of the camp were swiftly evacuated and taken over by the fighters. On the other three sides of the camp, the battle took place over stretches of waste ground, at longer range. Amal tanks were stationed around the camp behind buildings or huge piles of sand, moving forward to fire on the camp and then retreating out of sight. The Palestinians would shoot at them with rocket-propelled grenades during the few seconds they were in view. Thair and Ahmed told us that during the intense bombing on Saturday morning, 1,500 bombs fell on the camp in three hours. They also brought us things we needed. When the small stove, on which I made tea, ran out of gas, Ahmed came to the rescue with a little electric cooker from home.

The month of Ramadan ended June 8th but the fighting continued. On June 10th, six men were killed in two bomb explosions. I knew of course that Amal militiamen were being injured and killed as well, and we could sometimes hear the sirens of the ambulances taking their wounded to hospitals. "What a stupid war," I thought. "All this killing for these small camps full of refugees." But so much of the Lebanese civil war had been fought like this. Battles were waged and men died fighting for control of small districts, or single streets, sometimes even for one strategic building. And, as usual, those orchestrating the war were nowhere near the front lines.

On the morning of Wednesday, June 11, after more than three weeks of fighting, a ceasefire was declared, enabling the burial of the six dead from the day before. By the fridges to the side of the entrance hall of the hospital, the bodies were washed. Sixty to seventy women crowded in the entrance hall, singing, chanting and wailing their grief, and waving scarves. Two fainted with emotion and had to be revived. Erica and I stood amongst the women pushing up the stairs. I felt rather uncomfortable, as if I was intruding on a private ceremony, but friends came and stood with us and Erica explained that it was not an intrusion. To attend was to respect the dead. Later, at about 11.30 a.m., a message reached the hospital via the walkie-talkie that an Iranian delegation, accompanied by Hezbollah (Party of God) soldiers and maybe ten ambulances were entering the camp, having successfully negotiated with the Amal militia to be allowed to evacuate the wounded. Dr Rede thought it was prudent for Lieve, Dirk and I to stay out of sight, not because there was any direct danger to us in the camp, but because of the dangers of kidnapping outside the camp. It was probably better if we kept a low profile, he explained, as they did not know all the credentials of the Muslim fundamentalist soldiers accompanying the delegation and did not want us to be recognised on some other occasion outside Bourj al Barajneh. Rather disappointed, we waited in our room.

A TESTAMENT OF HOPE

DR MARTIN LUTHER KING JNR

National Civil Rights leader and Nobel Peace Prize winner Martin Luther King was born in 1929 and was assassinated in 1968. He was a young Baptist minister in Montgomery, Alabama, in 1955 when a black woman, Rosa Parks, was arrested for refusing to give up her bus seat to a white man. King and the other black leaders in Montgomery organized a boycott of the bus companies and eventually the state was forced to make segregated buses illegal.

A T THE CLOSE OF THE MEETING I asked the ministers to stay over for a few minutes to urge them to ride the buses during the rush hours for the first few days. It was our feeling that their presence would give the Negro citizens courage and make them less likely to retaliate in case of insults. The ministers readily agreed. Accordingly, two were assigned to each bus line in the city, to ride mainly during the morning and afternoon rush. They were given suggestions as to how to handle situations of violence and urged to keep an accurate record of all incidents.

I had decided that after many months of struggling with my people for the goal of justice I should not sit back and watch, but should lead them back to the buses myself. I asked Ralph Abernathy, E. D. Nixon, and Glenn Smiley to join me in riding on the first integrated bus. They reached my house around 5.45 on Friday morning. Television cameras, photographers, and news reporters were hovering outside the door. At 5.55 we walked toward the bus stop, the cameras shooting, the reporters bombarding us with questions. Soon the bus appeared; the door opened, and I stepped on. The bus driver greeted me with a cordial smile. As I put my fare in the box he said:

"I believe you are Reverend King, aren't you?"

I answered: "Yes I am."

"We are glad to have you this morning," he said.

I thanked him and took my seat, smiling now too. Abernathy, Nixon and Smiley followed, with several reporters and television men behind them. Glenn Smiley sat next to me. So I rode the first integrated bus in Montgomery with a white minister, and a native southerner, as my seatmate.

Downtown we transferred to one of the buses that

serviced the white residential section. As the white people
boarded, many took seats as if nothing were going on.
Others looked amazed to see Negroes sitting in front, and
some appeared peeved to know that they either had to sit
behind Negroes or stand. One elderly man stood up by the
conductor, despite the fact that there were several vacant
seats in the rear. When someone suggested to him that he
sit in back, he responded: "I would rather die and go to
hell than sit behind a nigger." A white woman
unknowingly took a seat by a Negro. When she noticed
her neighbour, she jumped up and said in a tone of
obvious anger: "What are these niggers gonna do next?"

But despite such signs of hostility there were no major
incidents on the first day. Many of the whites responded
to the new system calmly. Several deliberately and with
friendly smiles took seats beside Negroes. True, one Negro
woman was slapped by a white man as she alighted, but
she refused to retaliate. Later she said: "I could have

broken that little fellow's neck all by myself, but I left the mass meeting last night determined to do what Reverend King asked." The *Montgomery Advertiser* reported at the end of the first day: "The calm but cautious acceptance of this significant change in Montgomery's way of life came without any major disturbance."

But the reactionaries were not in retreat. Many of them had predicted violence, and such predictions are always a conscious or unconscious invitation to action. When people, especially in public office, talk about bloodshed as a concomitant of integration, they stir and arouse the hoodlums to acts of destruction, and often work under cover to bring them about. In Montgomery several public officials had predicted violence, and violence there had to be if they were to save face.

By December 28th the first few days of peaceful compliance had given way to a reign of terror. City buses were fired on throughout the city, especially in poorly lighted sections. A teenage girl was beaten by four or five white men as she alighted from a bus. A pregnant Negro woman was shot in the leg. Fearfully, many Negroes and whites refused to ride the buses. The city commission responded by suspending the night runs on city lines. No bus could begin a run after five o'clock, which meant that once again returning workers were without transportation. This was exactly what the violent elements wanted.

During this period a new effort was made to divide the Negroes. Handbills were distributed urging Negroes to rebel against me in particular and their leaders in general. These leaflets purported to come from "fed-up" Negroes, but virtually everyone knew that they were the work of white extremists. Referring to me as Luther, one leaflet said: "We get shot at while he rides. He is getting us in more trouble every day. Wake up. Run him out of town." Another one stated: "We have been doing OK in Montgomery before outside preachers were born! Ask

Reverend King's papa and mamma if they like his doings – ask him if they going to help in Atlanta. Better quit him before it is too late!"

The KKK [Ku Klux Klan] was in its element. One day it descended upon Montgomery in full regalia. But it seemed to have lost its spell. A college student who saw the Klansmen swarming the streets in their white costumes with red insignia went cheerfully on about her business, thinking that they were collecting for the United Fund. And one cold night a small Negro boy was seen warming his hands at a burning cross.

On January 9th, Ralph Abernathy and I went to Atlanta to prepare for a meeting of Negro leaders that I had called for the following day. In the middle of the night we were awakened by a telephone call from Ralph's wife, Juanita. I knew that only some new disaster would make her rouse us at two in the morning. When Ralph came back, his sober face told part of the story. "My home has been bombed," he said, "and three or four other explosions have been heard in the city, but Juanita doesn't know where yet." I asked about Juanita and their daughter. "Thank God, they are safe." Before we could talk any more, the telephone rang a second time. It was Juanita again, saying that the First Baptist Church had been hit. I looked at Ralph as he sat down beside me, stunned. Both his home and his church bombed in one night, and I knew no words to comfort him. There in the early morning hours we prayed to God together, asking for the power of endurance, the strength to carry on.

Between three and seven we received no less than fifteen calls. We finally learned that besides Ralph's home and church, Bob Graetz's home and three other Baptist churches – Bell Street, Hutchinson Street, and Mt Olive – had all been hit. Worrying that this time the people might be goaded into striking back, I called a few ministers in Montgomery and urged them to do what they could to keep control. In the meantime, Ralph and I arranged to fly

back, leaving the meeting of southern leaders to begin without us.

From Montgomery airport we drove directly to Ralph's house. The street was roped off, and hundreds of people stood staring at the ruins. The front porch had been almost completely destroyed, and things inside the house were scattered from top to bottom. Juanita, though shocked and pale, was fairly composed.

The rest of the morning was spent in a grim tour of the other bombings. The Bell Street and Mt Olive Baptist churches had been almost completely destroyed. The other two churches were less severely damaged, but nevertheless faced great losses. The total damage to the four churches was estimated at $70,000. Bob Graetz's home had been a bomb target the previous summer, but had escaped serious damage. This time he was not so fortunate. The front of his house lay in ruins, and shattered glass throughout the interior showed the violence of the explosion. Assembled at each of the bombed sites was a large group of angry people; but with a restraint that I never ceased to wonder at, they held themselves under control.

The next morning, three important white agencies issued statements condemning the bombings. Grover Hall, editor of the *Montgomery Advertiser*, wrote a strong editorial entitled "Is it safe to live in Montgomery?" in which he insisted that the issue had gone beyond the question of segregation versus integration. As I read Hall's strong statement I could not help admiring this brilliant but complex man who claimed to be a supporter of segregation but could not stomach the excesses performed in its name. Several white ministers denounced the bombing as unchristian and uncivilised, and all through the day their statement was repeated over television by the distinguished minister of the First Presbyterian Church, Rev. Merle Patterson. The Men of Montgomery, too, made known their unalterable opposition to the bombings. For the first time since the protest began, these influential whites were on public record on the side of law and order. Their stands gave us new confidence in the basic decency of the vast majority of whites in the community. Despite their commitment to segregation, it was clear that they were still law-abiding, and would never sanction the use of violence to preserve the system.

That afternoon, I returned to Atlanta to make at least an appearance at the meeting of Negro leaders. There I found an enthusiastic group of almost a hundred men from all over the South, committed to the idea of a southern movement to implement the Supreme Court's decision against bus segregation through nonviolent means. Before adjourning they voted to form a permanent organisation, the Southern Christian Leadership Conference, and elected me president, a position I still hold.

When I returned to Montgomery over the weekend I

found the Negro community in low spirits. After the bombings the city commission had ordered all buses off the streets; and it now appeared that the city fathers would use this reign of violence as an excuse to cancel the bus company's franchise. As a result, many were coming to feel that all our gains had been lost; and I myself started to fear that we were in for another long struggle to get bus service renewed. I was also beginning to wonder whether the virulent leaflets that were bombarding the Negro community might be having their effect. Discouraged, and still revolted by the bombings, for some strange reason I began to feel a personal sense of guilt for everything that was happening.

In this mood I went to the mass meeting on Monday night. There for the first time, I broke down in public. I had invited the audience to join me in prayer, and had begun by asking God's guidance and direction in all our activities. Then, in the grip of an emotion I could not control, I said, "Lord, I hope no one will have to die as a result of our struggle for freedom in Montgomery. Certainly I don't want to die. But if anyone has to die, let it be me." The audience was in an uproar. Shouts and cries of "no, no" came from all sides. So intense was the reaction, that I could not go on with my prayer. Two of my fellow ministers came to the pulpit and suggested that I take a seat. For a few minutes I stood with their arms around me, unable to move. Finally, with the help of my friends, I sat down. It was this scene that caused the press to report mistakenly that I had collapsed.

Unexpectedly, this episode brought me great relief. Many people came up to me after the meeting and many called the following day to assure me that we were all together until the end. For the next few days, the city was fairly quiet. Bus service was soon resumed, though still on a daytime schedule only.

Then another wave of terror hit. Early in the morning of 28 January, the People's Service Station and Cab Stand

was bombed, and another bomb fell at the home of Allen Robertson, a sixty-year-old Negro hospital worker. It was never discovered why these two victims had been singled out for attack. The same morning an unexploded bomb, crudely assembled from twelve sticks of dynamite, was found still smouldering on my porch.

I was staying with friends on the other side of town, and Coretta and "Yoki" were in Atlanta. So once more I heard the news first on the telephone. On my way home, I visited the other scenes of disaster nearby, and found to my relief that no one had been hurt. I noticed a police car driving away from the area with two Negroes on the rear seat. These men, I learned, were under arrest because they had challenged the police to their faces with having done nothing to catch the bombers. Both were later convicted of trying to "incite to riot." But there was no riot that day, although the crowds that gathered round the damaged buildings were once again ready for violence. They were just waiting for a signal. Fortunately, the signal never came.

At home I addressed the crowd from my porch, where the mark of the bomb was clear. "We must not return violence under any condition. I know this is difficult advice to follow, especially since we have been the victims of no less than ten bombings. But this is the way of Christ; it is the way of the cross. We must somehow believe that unearned suffering is redemptive." Then since it was Sunday morning, I urged the people to go home and get ready for church. Gradually they dispersed.

WOMAN IN THE MISTS

FARLEY MOWAT

American Dian Fossey led a long-term study into the behaviour of primates. She went to Africa in 1966 and high up in the Virungas, a kind of African rain-forest, she achieved amazing contact and friendship with mountain gorillas. At first she made inexperienced approaches to the animals but later became their friend. Tragedy struck when her favourite gorilla, Digit, was killed by poachers. Dian Fossey was murdered on 28 December 1985 by the human enemies she had made as a result of her battles for the protection of the gorillas. The following are extracts from Dian's journal.

I LEFT CAMP ALONE at 9.00. At 9.20 I heard a bark to the right, not far from the Bitshitsi trail.... It was Group 1... I take another few steps so as to be in the clearing when the animals see me, and I almost bump into the blackback male. I measure later; we were six feet apart. He stands up, blinks his eyes, opens his mouth, screams, and runs about fifty feet through the brush behind him, screaming and tearing at the undergrowth. There's quite a bit of screaming now from all sides, and a mother with infant, a juvenile, and an old female take to a tree. Old female and juvenile beat trees and chests and then juvenile runs to old female. Mother sits there holding branch with right arm and infant in left arm. She lets go of the branch and beats her chest, hitting the infant in the process. She stands up on the limb, wants to get down, but keeps looking at me hesitantly. Then in a split second she shoves the infant onto her back and leaps a good eight feet from the higher branch to a lower one covered with moss. She clings there for just a second with all four extremities and then leaps ten feet to the ground. As she lands, she gives a piercing scream and the infant lets out a long, high-pitched cry. I'm really worried about both of them, for it's not my intention to cause them harm. Just then the old female does the same thing, only when she reaches the lower branch she rolls off it and must have hit the ground on her back. She lets out a terrible scream and about four others in the bush join in.

Today Sanweke and I were charged by two gorillas and it wasn't a bluff charge – they really meant it. We were about one hundred and fifty feet directly downhill from a group when a silverback and a female decided to eradicate us. They gave us a split second of warning with screams and roars that seemed to come from every direction at once before they descended in a gallop that shook the ground. I was determined to stand fast, but when they broke through the foliage at a dead run directly above me, I felt my legs retreating in spite of what I've read about gorillas not charging fully. I paused long enough to try to dissuade them with my voice, which only seemed to aggravate them more, if possible; and when their long, yellow canines and wild eyes were no less than two feet away, I took a very ungainly nosedive into the thick foliage alongside the trail. They whizzed on by, caught up in their own momentum. It's a good thing they didn't come back to attack, for I was certainly in no position to defend myself. It may have taken only a split second to dive into that foliage, but it took about fifteen minutes to extract myself – what a tangle!

I've just about finished fixing up a room in the hut, and it looks great. The ugly wooden walls are matted with two-tone grass mats the natives made for me, and the wooden

supports are hidden by bamboo that was cut down the mountain a way and is a beautiful shade of moss green now. I have pictures, skins, tusks, and horns hanging here and there, and I've made curtains out of some African printed material. A fireplace will be built next week.

Work is going well, for I've been following one gorilla group around all month, and now I'm able to get within thirty to sixty feet of them and they are not afraid of me. To be perfectly frank, I think they are quite confused as to my species! I've gotten them accustomed to me by aping them, and they are fascinated by my facial grimaces and other actions that I wouldn't be caught dead doing in front of anyone. I feel like a complete fool, but this technique seems to be working, and because of the increased proximity I've been able to observe a lot never recorded before.

Last week two of them approached me to within twenty feet, and the rest of the group remained at thirty-five to sixty feet for over an hour! There aren't words to describe

what a thrill that was, and as long as I live I'll never forget it. At the same time I was slightly apprehensive because I was directly downhill from them and without a tree to climb or hide behind should anything have happened. I had to use my "threat face" once – don't laugh, it's quite effective – when one of the silverbacks began to get carried away with his bluffing tactics of running, chest beating, and breaking down trees. Needless to say, I was dutifully impressed with his prowess, but decided our proximity was being strained, so turned a horrible grimace on him, which had the effect of a flower on Ferdinand: immediately he sat down and began to eat, nervously and with one eye on me, but at least his hands were harmlessly occupied, and finally he just stood up and walked away.

When Dian's favourite gorilla, Digit, was killed by poachers, she wrote passionately to the President of the Rwanda Republic:

"You have had the kindness to show interest in the

gorillas of the Parc des Volcans. . . I'm sure you remember the gorilla who took my notebook and pen in the National Geographic movie and then returned them to me very gently before rolling over and going to sleep at my side. That same gorilla, named Digit, is also pictured on a big poster for Rwandan tourism saying 'Come and see me in Rwanda.' . . . On December 31st, Digit was speared to death by Rwandan poachers. They killed him, then cut off his head and hands and fled with them. . . These killers are all of the Commune of Mukingo. . . I would like to ask that they receive full punishment for their crimes. . . I would have given my life to have saved Digit's life, but it is too late for that now."

Writing to Dr Snider at the National Geographic she was less restrained. "Poachers have never before dared attack any of my working groups and I am now wondering if this is the beginning of the end. . . for if they get away with this killing, how much longer are the others going to last? I feel. . . that probably most of the gorillas on the other mountains, barring Mikeno, have been killed off by now for heads and hands. . . I can assure you I've done nothing illegal in retribution for Digit's death, but I am not allowing myself to think about how he must have suffered. . . My plan of action is to publicise the affair as strongly and graphically as possible to every conservation society I can reach to ask them to apply pressure onto the Rwanda government to threaten to cut the vast amounts of money coming in to the Parc des Volcans for guards and a conservateur who do NOT work at protection of the park – that work is done by this camp – and to put pressure on the government to enforce extreme penalties for poachers – either prolonged imprisonment or death, and to allow guards to kill poachers within the park."

Her diary continues.

Just as we were about to start the autopsy, my woodman,

working about fifty feet from my house, began yelling in Swahili, "Poachers! Poachers!" The houseman ran into the cabin screaming the same. The woodman had seen a poacher with bow and arrows just on the fringe of the camp area.

No poachers have dared come near my camp for at least three years! But now they've nearly exterminated all of the antelope within the rest of the park and the only place where antelope now flourish is here. If they could get away with killing a gorilla in the study area, why not antelopes at camp?

I yelled to my camp staff to chase the poachers while I grabbed my gun (not legally registered) and ran after them, leaving the two Europeans, who just sat there stunned. I kept running and shooting up in the air to keep him from crossing the main open meadows above camp where he could have disappeared into the forested areas and never have been found. My men, including Vatiri, Nemeye, and Kanyarangna, could then squeeze him up against the slopes of Visoke, which is what they did, and captured him there along with a bloodstained bow and five arrows.

He was a baby-faced little Twa and one of Digit's killers, as he admitted. Both the front and back of his tattered yellow shirt were sprayed with fountains of Digit's dried blood. We were a good hour catching him. I'm really proud of my men, and I haven't run like that myself since I was ten years old!

We brought him back to camp and tied him up, and my Africans began to "question" him while we went on with poor Digit's autopsy. It was a gruesome business in that the spears and pangas had pierced so many of his organs – lungs, heart, spleen, intestines, and stomach. When we finished, we three went inside my cabin for a bit of lunch that nobody felt like eating. While this was being prepared, my Africans were outside with the Twa examining him.

We hadn't been in five minutes when all hell broke loose and my men began screaming "poacher" again. I thought the original prisoner had escaped and dashed outside, but in actual fact three of his accomplices had crept up to look for him and were seen by my men. By this time the Europeans were almost basket cases. My Africans and I began another chase, but I had to give up, though they followed the tracks for another two hours without result.

I returned to camp to guard the Twa. By this time the Europeans seemed extraordinarily anxious to depart, so I brought the Twa inside and hogtied him to the beams for a lengthy period of questioning. I did nothing terribly illegal, though my men and I examined him very very very thoroughly. I can't say how difficult it was for me not to kill him when he admitted having been one of Digit's killers. I asked two of my Africans to spend the night sleeping on each side of him. I could not trust myself alone with that thing.

We "interviewed" him until quite late at night, and during the course of our interrogation we obtained the names of *all* Digit's killers. The chief ones were Munyarukiko, Gashabizi, Ntanyungu, Rubanda, and Runyaga, all from Mukingo commune.

What stunned me almost more than anything was the motive for Digit's death. A Hutu merchant had offered to pay the head poacher, Munyarukiko, the equivalent of twenty dollars to get the head and hands of a silverback. Digit was a young silverback. The Hutu hoped to find a tourist who would pay him much more for the souvenirs. This man has succeeded in obtaining a number of gorilla heads and hands previously to sell to tourists. The Twa prisoner told us he knew where Digit's head and hands were buried, near Munyarukiko's house under a clump of bamboo.

Next day I sent down a message to the *chef des brigades*, Paulin Nkubili, saying we'd caught one of Digit's killers and that I would *not* release him to the park guards, who have a way of "losing" their prisoners. Therefore on the seventh, Nkubili climbed to camp, accompanied by three commandos. They repeated the interrogation, but didn't learn anything my men and I hadn't already gathered.

Finally I allowed them to take the Twa down to a military security compound, where he is being held awaiting presidential decree as to the extent of his punishment. Nkubili seemed somewhat afraid of me. I can't imagine why.

I can say that to let the Twa go was one of the most difficult things I've ever done in my life. It was only in respect of Digit's memory that he left here untouched.

It now appears that many of the Virunga gorillas have recently been killed off by poachers. The only abundant population remaining consists of my study groups. This could be the beginning of the end of the remaining two hundred or so mountain gorillas. Only if I can elicit enough interest and support can their total decimation be prevented.

Three years later, having been back in America, Dian returned to her beloved gorillas.

To reach them meant a long climb lasting two hours and filled with such oaths from me that the long-dormant volcanoes should have erupted, because a new tracker, Kana, took the most energy-wasting and zigzag route. We finally found them in a bowl between First and Second hills south of camp. Kana headed back right away, leaving me huffing and puffing like a run-out old buffalo.

The females and youngsters of the clan (sixteen in all) were resting in thick vegetation in the warm sun on the steep slope of the bowl where they had made their day nests. When I got my breath, I worked my way down toward them, though I could see only the occasional one. When I got twenty feet from them I sat down and began making Fossey-style introduction noises – a soft series of

rumbles like gorillas make when expressing contentment.

The nearest female was old Effie, mother of six, whom I had known since 1967. She'd had a new baby in my absence, little Maggie, who sure didn't believe in making shy. Maggie came scrambling over right away – not to look at me, but to investigate my clothing and equipment. This dismayed me because I thought it was the result of too much habituation with the tourists the park gang has kept on sending to Group 5.

But my dismay only lasted a second or two. Effie glanced my way while chewing on a stalk of celery. She looked away, then did a double-take myopic scrutiny as if not believing her eyes. Then she tossed the celery aside and began walking rapidly toward me.

Meantime Tuck, another female I had known nearly as long, appeared out of the underbrush and started to pick up Maggie, I guess to take her off to safety, then Tuck too did a second take. She dropped Maggie and walked right up in front of me, resting her weight on her arms so that her face was level with mine and only a couple of inches away. She stared intently into my eyes, and it was eye-to-eye contact for thirty or forty seconds. Not knowing quite what to do, for I had never had this reaction from gorillas before, I squished myself flat on the bed of vegetation. Whereupon she smelled my head and neck, then lay down beside me... and embraced me!... embraced me!... embraced me! GOD, she *did* remember!

Tuck began crooning, and I crooned back. Effie had come up by then and she too stared straight into my eyes, sniffed me, then piled up on the two of us and I was really squished. Her and Tuck's plaintive murmurs reached other clan members in the dense foliage nearby, and one by one the other females came over to us. All the older four that I knew best repeated the eye-to-eye contact, then settled down with long arms entwining all of us into one big, black, furry ball. As they settled in, each one was making prolonged, inquisitive "hmmmmm" sounds as if to ask: "Where the hell have you been? Is this really you?"

Not to be left out, the youngsters joined us too: Jozi, Cantsbee, Pablo, and Maggie really took advantage of the trust their mothers were showing to work me over, gently hitting, nibbling, pinching me, and pulling my hair, and trying to carry off everything loose. They tried to take my camera, water jug, panga, and my glasses, which, unfortunately, I have to wear in the field now. They did kidnap my new leather gloves (two hours later I found the right one, but the left one is forever on the mountain).

I could have happily died right then and there and wished for nothing more on earth, simply because they had remembered.

While the kids cavorted a few feet from us, Effie, Puck, Poppy, Tuck, and I settled down to enjoy a forty-five-minute palaver, all nestled up together amidst the thistle and celery clumps. I'm ashamed to say I did most of the vocalizing, but with an audience like this how could I resist?

While we ladies had our confab, old Beethoven, the leader of the group, with the two blackbacks Ziz and Shinda, fed their way down into the bottom of the bowl, paying us no heed. The other silverback, Icarus, stayed on our slope about fifteen feet from the ladies' gossip circle but didn't interrupt. Eventually Beethoven looked up at us and barked that the party was over. Time to go. The ladies and their offspring moved off slowly, leaving me with absolute disbelief at what had happened. They *knew* me – they *welcomed* me back! Perhaps they were even happy to see the Lone Woman of the Forest again.

I tried to visit them next day, but they had returned to the high part of the saddle, about eleven thousand feet and five hours' walk away. I couldn't make it.

Later, while walking toward the Zaire border with Kana her tracker, Dian made another contact.

This time it was with Tiger, now a lone silverback, whom I had observed on the day of his birth in November 1967. He was born into Group 4, the group that was decimated by poachers in 1978. Since then he has had rather a tough time. For a time he batched it with some of the other surviving Group 4 males, but for three years he has been travelling alone, trying to find some females with whom to mate and start a clan of his own. This means "interactions" with the silverbacks of other groups, in which he has been rather badly beaten up despite his tremendous size and strength.

Even though I have known him since his birth, when I found him this time near the old cattle path I was following, I did not expect the kind of reception I had received from Group 5, because he is a lone animal, and they tend to be temperamental and unpredictable.

When I spotted him he was about fifty feet away, feeding in dense foliage, most of which was celery. I motioned Kana to go and hide, which he was glad to do

because Tiger is one big gorilla! I then sat down to give all the proper gorilla introduction vocalizations and quickly get my camera out of my knapsack, though I was sure I wouldn't get any pictures because he would flee as soon as he realised someone was near.

I had just barely taken the camera from the bag when – zoooom – he came right at me at a loping run. Reaching my side he lopped down a big lobelia with one hand, then raised his arm again as if he was going to whack the @$%& out of me! Then, to my relief, he slowly lowered his arm and gently stroked my arm before sitting on the base of a tree not two feet from my side.

There he sat gazing down at me, seeking eye contact, and for about fifteen minutes we exchanged "remarks" in groans, grunts and croons while I also took picture after picture. The reason for all the pictures was that I couldn't see him clearly without my glasses, but he might not have known me with glasses on, so a compromise had to be reached. I could see him through the viewfinder, in fact I could have counted the hairs on his great big head!

My tracker was nervous, since he was only fifty feet away, and he cracked a branch. Tiger swung over there to investigate, and Kana went back to camp somewhat hastily! After that Tiger and I spent the rest of the afternoon together, munching celery stalks and just keeping each other company.

When heavy fog and rain moved in at four-thirty I had to go, but felt great compunction about leaving him alone in the forest. I half expected him to follow me home and half wished he would. Poor "little" fellow. It was really quite sad as every now and then he would gaze over in the direction of Karisimbi and give one or two plaintive hoots as if bewailing his sad, lonely single status. My anger at the poachers who destroyed his family kept me cussing all the way back to camp.

ESCAPE FROM COLDITZ

from Colditz – The Full Story

The prisoners in Colditz Castle in Germany during the Second World War were regarded as an elite – they had all escaped from other prisoner of war camps and been recaptured with considerable difficulty. Colditz was a medieval fortress built high on a cliff, surrounded by a moat and vast quantities of barbed wire. Spotlights weaved around its perimeters every night and the castle should have been escape-proof. But with resourceful characters like Pat Reid around – it wasn't.

A T MORNING *APPELL* [roll-call] on October 15th no less than ten British officers were found to be missing. This is what had happened.

Dick Howe had come to me towards the end of September to tell me of a scheme hatched by Ronnie Littledale and Billie Stephens. The idea was to sortie from one of the windows of the kitchen over the low roofs of various store buildings in the adjoining *Kommandantur* [the German quarters] courtyard (which were in full view of all the windows of the *Kommandantur* above the ground floor), descend to the ground and cross the path of a sentry when his back was turned. The next thing was to crawl across the dimly lit area in front of the *Kommandantur* to a small open pit visible from the POW windows. At this point the escapers would still be in the bosom of the enemy, yet the plan went no further! I said the scheme was lunatic, but Dick confessed he wanted to let them have a shot. "And I want you to go with them, just to see they don't get into any trouble." I could see no prospect other than another month in the cooler, but I thought I might as well agree to join them.

I wondered if it would be possible to break into the tall block of buildings from which Dominic Bruce had escaped on 8 September. Bruce was doing his resulting solitary at the time, but I smuggled a message to him with his food and in due course had an answer. He pointed out that once inside this building one could descend from unbarred windows on the far side into the Castle's moat. The top floors were empty, but Germans occupied the floors below. There was a large door into the building which led to an unused staircase, but it was visible from almost everywhere and in full view of the *Kommandantur* sentries. This door was also locked (albeit not with a cruciform device). It was true that the floodlights at night threw the doorway into shadow, but the main thoroughfare from the outer Castle gateway to the entrance of the *Kommandantur* passed within a yard of it.

Using a stooge I entered the kitchen and examined the window giving on to the flat roofs. Working on four successive evenings I sawed through the head of a rivet on one of the bars (taking enormous care not to alert a sentry on his beat a mere fifteen yards away), and on the fifth evening removed the rivet itself with a silent working punch made for me by Wally Hammond. Once the rivet was removed, the bar could be bent back to allow a man to squeeze through the window. I camouflaged the joint with a clay rivet.

I invited Hank Wardle to join us (he agreed we hadn't a chance), making a party of four. A further six men would be concealed about the Castle as ghosts to cover our escape. We four all had our identity papers, general maps, money and compass, kept usually in our 'creepers'. The map of the Singen border-crossing into Switzerland we had to commit to memory – I had forbidden frontier maps to be carried many months before. Clothes had long since been prepared. I had one of my cloth caps, converted RAF trousers, a windjacket and a German civilian overcoat which I had bought off a French officer who had obtained it from a French orderly who in turn had access to the village. I also had a pair of black shoes.

Hank and I decided to pose as Flemish workmen collaborating with the Germans. As *Flammands* we could pass off our bad German and our bad French, and we would be unlikely to run into someone who spoke Flemish. We constructed elaborate case-histories.

We also carried cardboard (ersatz leather) suitcases which had been sent for from Britain containing Army clothing. The value of a suitcase was that a man without one travelling across Germany on main-line expresses looked like a fugitive. It would be hell lugging them out of the camp, but well worth the effort in the end. We would need to wrap them in blankets to muffle sound; in any case, we were to take enough sheets and blankets to make a fifty-foot descent.

After evening *Appell* on October 14th we all made the highly dangerous run to the kitchen; Malcolm McColm was with us to cover our traces. Balaclava helmets and gloves covered our white skins.

Hank and I got through the window, made our way across the low roofs and dropped to the ground. A British orchestra – which the Germans had had several nights to get used to – was playing in the *Saalhaus* [a wing of the castle], conducted by Douglas Bader. Bader had a clear view of the sentry for the whole of his beat. The idea was to use the music for signalling: when they stopped playing it meant the escapers could cross his path.

The orchestra was playing as arranged, but each time I
started across on the cessation of the music, it started
again. Then I heard German voices. It was the duty officer
on his rounds. Suspicious, he was questioning the sentry.
Five minutes later the music stopped again, but this time I
was caught napping, and I dared not risk a late dash. I
waited a long time and the music did not begin again.
Obviously things had gone wrong for the orchestra. I
decided to wait an hour, to let suspicions die down.

In the hope that we could hide in that time from any
passing Goon, I tried the handle of a door in the angle of
the wall where we were hiding. It opened, and we entered
warily. It was pitch-black inside. We went through a
second door and took refuge in a room which seemed to
contain no more than rubbish.

When the hour was up, we crept out again, and moved
to the end of the wall as the sentry's footsteps indicated

that he was turning on his beat. I peered round the corner, saw the soldier ten yards off marching away, and with Hank close behind tiptoed across the pathway (we wore socks over our shoes). Soon we were hiding in a small shrubbery near the entrance to the *Kommandantur*. Ronnie and Billie clambered across the roofs from the kitchen when they saw us cross the path, and in no time we were all in the pit.

My next job was to see if I could open the door into the building from which Dominic Bruce had escaped. It was fifteen yards away. I reached it, and apart from a hair-raising interruption when I heard Priem [the principal camp officer] returning from an evening in the town, I worked for an hour without success. We would have to find another way out.

A tunnel led from our pit under a verandah. We felt our way along until we came to a cellar. At the far end was an air-vent or chimney flue. At first it seemed impossible for a man to negotiate this shaft, but after a few moments of despair I found that by removing some of my clothing I could slide up easily enough. I could see that it led to a barred opening at the level of the ground outside – that is, on the far side of the building, where lay the moat for which we were heading. One of the bars was loose in its mortar socket; I freed one end and bent it nearly double. We could just squeeze through!

It was an enormous struggle, and we each had to strip naked, but by 3.30 a.m. we were all lying in bushes on the moat side of the *Kommandantur*. Indeed we were on the very edge of the moat. We peered over. Luckily the moat wall was stepped into three successive descents; the drops were about twelve feet and the steps were about two yards wide. We made a couple of sheet-ropes and climbed down, fully clothed once more. It was 4.30 a.m. By 5.15 a.m. we were over the outer boundary wall – none too soon, because we had a long way to go before dawn.

Eggers [assistant to Priem] was in Dresden attending a

conference called to discuss the use of as many POWs as possible in German industry, a need arising out of the heavy losses Germany was suffering on the eastern front:

I returned from Dresden on October 15th and found all passengers being checked by the police when I changed trains at Dobeln. My heart sank. I knew without asking. "Yes," they said. "Four prisoners missing from that *verdammten Sonderlager* of yours!"

That morning four British officers had been found missing after the usual hullabaloo.

Once again it was a report from a civilian coming up through the *Tiergarten* [the gardens surrounding the castle] which had warned us that something was up. She had found some suspicious blue and white material (the usual bedsheets) under some bushes.

Although they found plenty of evidence to indicate the route we had taken, they simply could not believe that we could have done so and not been seen by the sentry. Eventually they concluded that somehow or other we had escaped via the *Saalhaus*.

News of the record-breaking success of the four escapers in reaching Switzerland became known in Colditz – according to Platt's diary – on November 9th. Hank and I crossed the Swiss frontier on October 18th, a Sunday night. Billie and Ronnie arrived safely over the frontier the following evening at 10.30 p.m.

On October 23rd, Colonel Breyer of the OKW, Leipzig, visited Colditz with the object of showing two high-ranking Italian officers, in typically festooned flamboyant uniform, around the prison. Eggers records that they realized this would provide a festive occasion for the POWs. In fact, the Italians had already been spotted from a prison window and loud cries of "Macaroni" were already wafting into the *Kommandantur*. Eggers persuaded the *Kommandant* to show the visitors around the outside of the Castle only.

News concerning the men who escaped successfully from Colditz in 1941 and 1942 trickled into the camp slowly, and was sketchy when it arrived, to say the least of it. Nevertheless, when it came it boosted the prisoners' morale considerably. A first wave of elation started about a week after an escape, when, with the continued absence of the escapers and glum reactions from the Germans upon questioning by the SBO [Senior British Officer] as to their whereabouts, it was reasonably safe to assume that the men were out of enemy territory, provided they had not been killed en route.

Reliable confirmation arrived by various routes: sometimes a picture postcard slipped through the censor's net, written in a disguised hand from a fictitious character, but leaving no uncertainty in the mind of the recipient as to the meaning of the seemingly innocuous phrases in the text.

Hank Wardle, often called Murgatroyd by Rupert Barry, thus wrote to him from Switzerland in November 1942:

We are having a holiday here (in Switzerland) and are sorry you are not with us. Give our dear love to your friend Dick. Love from
Harriette and Phyllis Murgatroyd

"Harriette" and "Phyllis", with the H and P heavily emphasised, were obvious cover-names for Hank and Pat.

"ADDLED YOUTH"

RONALD W. CLARK

from Edison: The Man Who Made the Future

Thomas Alva Edison (1847-1931) was a tireless inventor, constantly investigating the possibilities of electricity and developing new ideas and devices. During his life he patented over 1000 inventions including the electric light bulb and the phonograph (the predecessor of the gramophone). As this extract shows, his ingenuity was apparent from the very beginning.

I N 1854 THE EDISONS moved to Fort Gratiot on the outskirts of Port Huron, more than 100 miles north of their previous home and on the southern tip of Lake Huron.

Soon after the move north Tom Edison caught scarlet fever and it was not until 1855, at the age of eight and a half, that he began attending the white school house. Here he showed what has almost become a sign of genius: after only three months he returned home in tears, reporting that the teacher had described him as "addled". This was in fact no cause for alarm. Leonardo da Vinci, Hans Andersen and Neils Bohr were all singled out in their youth as cases of retarded development; Newton was considered a dunce; the teacher of Sir Humphry Davy commented, "While he was with me I could not discern the faculties by which he was so much distinguished"; and Einstein's headmaster was to warn that the boy "would never make a success of anything." As youths, all had one characteristic in common: each was an individualist, saw no need to explain himself and was thus listed among the odd men out.

Whether Nancy Edison took the Port Huron schoolteacher's opinion seriously or whether she rightly believed herself a better teacher than the local man is a moot point. But Edison remembered the outcome for the rest of his life.

I found out what a good thing a mother was, she brought me back to the school and angrily told the teacher that he didn't know what he was talking about. She was the most enthusiastic champion a boy ever had, and I determined right then that I would be worthy of her, and show her that her confidence had not been misplaced.

Family loyalty and affection no doubt played its part in recollection. Nevertheless, it is from the age of seven, when mother takes over, that the story of the young Edison begins to diverge from that of his contemporaries. By the age of nine he had read Richard Green Parker's *Natural and Experimental Philosophy* and at the age of thirteen he discovered the writings of Thomas Paine on his father's bookshelves. Almost three-quarters of a century later he wrote:

It was a revelation to me to read that great thinker's views on political and theological subjects. Paine educated me then about many matters on which I had never before thought. I remember very vividly the flash of enlightenment that shone from Paine's writings... My interest in Paine and his writings was not satisfied by my first reading of his works. I went back to them time and again, just as I have done since my boyhood days.

He also struggled through Newton's *Principia*. It was important in giving him the respect for practice rather than theory which explains both his success as an inventor and the slowness with which the world of science recognized his achievements. Newton's masterpiece, however, helped to give him an almost arrogant contempt for mathematics, an attitude not entirely balanced by his skill in seeing intuitively to the heart of many problems based on figures. A family friend helped to explain the *Principia* in simple language. The result, according to Edison was:

[I] at once came to the conclusion that Newton could have dispensed his knowledge in a much wider field had he known less about figures. It gave me a distaste for mathematics from which I never recovered. . . I look upon figures as mathematical tools which are employed to carve out the logical result of reasoning, but I do not consider them necessary to assist one to an intelligent understanding of the result.

Years afterward he was to claim: "I am not a mathematician, but I can get within ten percent in the higher reaches of the art." And, with more truth but more arrogance: "I can always hire mathematicians, but they can't hire me."

That Edison was to reach a position in the financial pecking order so much above that of most mathematicians was due largely to his practice of relentless practical experiment, begun in the basement of his Port Huron home in the 1850s as he worked his way through the pages of *Natural and Experimental Philosophy*, repeating the author's experiments to confirm that what Parker said would happen, actually did happen.

For a boy of his native energy and instinctive curiosity about the natural world, it was a good decade in which to be young. During the early years of the century André Marie Ampère, Karl Friedrich Gauss and Georg Ohm had begun to disentangle the links connecting electricity and magnetism, first definitively shown by Hans Christian Oersted's earlier observation of the deflection of a compass needle by a nearby electric current. Michael Faraday suggested that the phenomena of electricity and magnetism could best be considered in terms of fields, or areas of space over which their forces were exercised, and James Clerk Maxwell was soon preparing his revolutionary theory that neither electricity nor magnetism existed in isolation, and working at his equations which linked the two phenomena.

Building on this theoretical work, inventors had already harnessed the newly understood force of electricity to create the glaring arc light, limited in use but already giving spectacular results, as in Paris where the Place de la Concorde was lit by the luminous discharge between sputtering carbon rods. In America, where the arc was already blazing out its glaring light, Samuel Morse had patented an electromagnetic device by which messages in the dots and dashes of his eponymous code could be sent along metal wires. In 1844 the words "What hath God wrought" had been tapped out along a wire between Washington and Baltimore and three years later New York had been connected by the telegraph to Washington.

All these achievements had come, if not directly from the scientists who had shown them to be theoretically possible, then at least from their close collaborators. Research and development, in its modern sense, had been minimal or non-existent, and sheer wonder at the arc light or the telegraph had been enough to push them into immediate use. If this was one explanation of the primitive quality which typified the equipment of the emerging technological world, another was that the development of materials and techniques for specific scientific purposes was still in its infancy. Any young man of the 1850s, glimpsing even a small part of the landscape then opening up, could well have felt like Kipling's explorer who

heard the milewide mutterings of unimagined rivers,
And beyond the nameless timber saw illimitable plains.

Edison was lucky. As it was written in 1926, had he been born into early twentieth-century America, "he would probably have become professor of a technical institute, or a technical employee in a Trust," impeded by regulations and financial dependence from achieving greatness.

In the less disciplined, less hidebound, world of the 1860s, he had first to find out what was really known: to understand and to observe; to be perpetually asking the most difficult question of all – "why?" He did this, and more, as he repeated Parker's textbook experiments in the cellar of his parents' Port Huron house. He scrounged bottles from the local shopkeepers and later remembered that there were eventually 200 of them, each filled with a different chemical. Near explosions and near disasters almost inevitably followed. Most were looked upon by the boy's parents not only with worry and a fear about what might happen next, but also pride that their boy could even begin to understand such things. "Addled," indeed!

He soon grew ambitious. The Grand Trunk Railroad had in 1859 completed a line from Portland, Maine, to Sarnia, on the eastern side of the St Clair River, opened a car ferry between Sarnia and Port Huron on the Western bank of the river, and simultaneously completed a single-track line which ran south from Port Huron to Detroit. This suggested possibilities and Edison eventually persuaded his mother to let him apply for a post as newsboy on the morning train from Port Huron to Detroit. He partly persuaded her that he was really grown up, it is asserted, with the announcement: "Ma! I'm a bushel of wheat! I weigh eighty pounds." The story, though told by Edison himself, has an apocryphal ring; nevertheless, like most such stories, it is based on an underlying foundation. It might not be correct as one of Edison's hagiographers was later to claim, that even at this early age, his "mind was an electric thunderstorm rushing through the fields of truth." But by the time he was twelve he had begun to quantify the facts of everyday life.

The morning train left Port Huron at 7 a.m. and covered the sixty-three miles to Detroit in four hours; left for home at 5.30 p.m. and arrived back at 9.30. To the young Edison the advantages of working the $14^1/_2$-hour day were twofold. Although as newsboy he would earn only what he could make from paper sales, the concession of candy butcher went with the job, and to a boy of Edison's imagination there was no limit to what he might earn from sales of sweets and food. There was also the six hours' stopover in Detroit which could be spent in the reading room of the Young Men's Association, soon to be reorganized as the Detroit Free Library.

He quickly began to show a sure business instinct. On the morning trip into the city he sold fruit and other local produce from Port Huron, doing it so successfully that he soon had other boys working for him. The evening papers were sold on the trip back and within a few months profit was running at twenty dollars a week.

Next, he was supplementing business with vegetables

from the large garden surrounding his parents' home. "After being on the train for several months," he once said, "I started two stores in Port Huron – one for periodicals, and the other for vegetables, butter and berries in the season. They were attended by two boys who shared in the profits."

He had barely launched this venture when he began to go deaf. According to the earliest published accounts of his life it was the result of a severe boxing round the ears by the train guard, a story which he appears at one time to have endorsed. Later in life he said that he had been delayed by a group of newspaper customers and the train had began to pull away from the platform without him.

I ran after it and caught the rear step nearly out of wind and hardly able to lift myself up, for the steps in those days were high [he recalled]. A trainman reached and grabbed me by the ears and as he pulled me up I felt something in my ears crack and right after that I began to get deaf. . . . If it was that man who injured my hearing, he did it while saving my life.

First there was earache, then a slight difficulty in hearing, finally a deafness that was to become permanent and worse as he grew older. The real cause is still something of a mystery. The after-effects of scarlet fever have been suggested, so has inheritance, and it is certainly true that Edison suffered from ear troubles throughout a long life, and was twice operated on for mastoids.

It is a measure of his character that he turned to advantage what for most boys would have been a major handicap. Since he was still able to converse with people without too much trouble, since it was the subtleties of music rather than its basic sounds which escaped him, it is clear that the deafness was qualified. Nevertheless, it was hardness of hearing – possibly a more accurate description than deafness in the early days – that drove him to find consolation in the Detroit library even more regularly. Here, he would often recall, he started with the first book on the bottom shelf and worked his way along until the shelf was finished and he could start on the next one.

The disability was also to help with his professional work, even during his early days as a telegraph operator. "While I could hear unerringly the loud ticking of the instrument," he later recalled, "I could not hear other and perhaps distracting sounds. I could not even hear the instrument of the man next to me in a big office."

Later still, when he was developing Bell's early telephone, his difficulty in hearing its faint sounds convinced him of the need for improvements; the outcome was the all-important carbon transmitter, an essential of the instrument even today.

As for the gramophone, Edison was to have no doubts. "Deafness, pure and simple, was responsible for the experimentation which perfected the machine. It took me twenty years to make a perfect record of piano music because it is full of overtones. I now can do it – just because I'm deaf." There was, moreover, one other advantage in defective hearing. In the business jungle

where Edison necessarily carried out much of his business he could not rely on verbal agreements; everything had to be in writing, a safety net in what has been called "a business era notorious for financial swindle and brigandage."

At the time of the early deafness he was a plumpish round-faced youngster, a boy of twelve much like his companions except for inexhaustible energy and an audacity that usually overrode opposition. He used a spare freight car on the daily run as his own travelling laboratory and, without a by-your-leave, used the same car as his own printing works after acquiring a hand printing press and begging sufficient type from a friend on the *Detroit Free Press*. The result, appearing soon afterward, was the *Grand Trunk Herald* of which Edison printed 400 copies a week. According to some stories, laboratory and press were eventually thrown off the car after the chemicals had caused a fire.

My copy [he would recall] was so purely local that outside the cars
and the shops I don't suppose it interested a solitary human being.
But I was very proud of my bantling, and looked upon myself as a
simon-pure newspaper man. My items used to run like this: "John
Robinson, baggage master at James's Creek Station, fell off the
platform yesterday and hurt his leg. The boys are sorry for John." Or
it might be: "No. 3 Burlington engine has gone into the shed for
repairs."

There were also more exciting items as when he
reported, under "Births": "At Detroit Junction G.T.R.
Refreshment Rooms on the 22nd inst., the wife of A. Little,
of a daughter."

Edison's *Grand Trunk Herald* was an omen of many
things to come since it brought him into the newspapers
for the first time. George Stephenson, the British engineer,
made an extensive inspection of the line and was reported
by the London *Times* as having commented on the Edison
publication – the first newspaper to be produced on a train
as he described it.

Shortly afterwards there came an incident that
illustrated three traits that were to run through the whole
of Edison's life and that were symptomatic of his age.
They were quickness at turning chance circumstance to his
own benefit, a refusal to be deterred, and a relentlessness –
some would say a ruthlessness – in exacting as much
payment for a job as the traffic would stand.

One of his main problems had been to estimate
accurately how many papers he would sell on the Detroit–
Port Huron run each evening. If he carried too few he
could lose business; if he carried too many he could end
up with unsold stock. To minimize the risk he persuaded a
compositor on the *Detroit Free Press* to show him a proof of
the paper's main news story each day. Thus warned, he
could estimate what the sales on the home run were likely
to be.

Then, on an afternoon in early April 1862, his friend
showed him the proof of a sensational front page story.

The Civil War was already a year old and now Grant and Sherman had met in a huge and bloody battle at Shiloh near Corinth, Tennessee. The Confederates had lost General Albert S. Johnston and although the battle was still raging and the issue still in doubt, killed and wounded were already reported to number 25,000.

"I grasped the situation at once," Edison recalled. "Here was a chance for enormous sales, if only the people along the line could know what had happened. If only they could see the proof slip I was then reading! Suddenly an idea occurred to me." First he made for the telegraph operator on the Detroit station. Would he, Edison asked, telegraph to each of the main stations down the line and suggest that the station master should chalk up the news of the battle on the boards usually carrying the train times. In return Edison offered to supply the man with *Harper's Weekly*, *Harper's Monthly*, and an evening paper for the next six months. That bargain struck, he went to the *Free Press* offices and asked for 1,500 copies on credit. On being

refused he talked his way into the office of the editor, Wilbur F. Storey, who listened to his request in silence. Then he handed the boy a slip of paper, saying: "Take that downstairs and you will get what you want."

I took my fifteen hundred papers, got three boys to help me fold them, and mounted the train, all agog to find out whether the telegraph operator had kept his word [Edison remembered]. At the town where our first stop was made I usually sold two papers. As the train swung into that station, I looked ahead, and thought there must be a riot going on. A big crowd filled the platform, and as the train drew up I began to realize that they wanted my papers. Before we left I had sold a hundred or two at five cents a piece. At the next station the place was fairly black with people. I raised the ante, and sold three hundred papers at *ten* cents each. So it went on until Port Huron was reached. Then I transferred my remaining stock to the wagon which always waited for me there, hired a small boy to sit on the pile of papers in the back of the wagon, so as to discount any pilfering, and sold out every paper I had at a quarter of a dollar or more per copy. I remember I passed a church full of worshippers and stopped to yell out my news. In ten seconds there was not a soul left in the meeting. All of them, including the parson, were clustered round me, bidding against each other for copies of the precious paper.

You can understand why it struck me then that the telegraph must be about the best thing going, for it was the telegraphic notices on the bulletin boards which had done the trick. I determined at once to become a telegraph operator.

Yet, there was more to it than that. The Civil War had broken out just as the telegraph had begun to revolutionize civilian life, and it had quickly become evident to both sides that it could also revolutionize war. As the commanders of the manoeuvring armies began to realize how the telegraph both enlarged their sources of intelligence and strengthened their links with officers in the field, first scores, then hundreds, of telegraph operators became attached to the marching and countermarching forces. The Union Army alone eventually had 1,500 on its payroll. As the demand rose the supply diminished. Thus the profession had a doubly romantic attraction: participation in a war in which both sides fought for strongly held beliefs, and in a new science with a great future.

Thus a man of Edison's push and verve might well have become an operator whatever the chances of Fate. As it was, he took the first step following a storybook illustration of the young boy-hero at work.

A few months after the Battle of Shiloh had brought him a relative fortune, the mixed train from Port Huron to Detroit, carrying both freight and passengers, stopped at Mt Clemens for the half-hour during which shunting had to take place. Edison was already friendly with the red-bearded station agent, J. U. Mackenzie, and Mackenzie's two-and-a-half-year-old son, Jimmy.

The train, of some twelve or fifteen freight cars, had pulled ahead and had backed in upon the freight-house siding, had taken out a box car (containing ten tons of handle material for Jackson State prison), and had pushed it with sufficient momentum to reach the baggage car without a brakeman controlling it [Mackenzie later recalled]. Al, who had been admiring the fowls in the poultry yard, happened to turn at this moment and notice little Jimmy on the main track, throwing pebbles over his head in the sunshine, utterly unconscious of the danger he was in. Al dashed his papers (which was under his arm) upon the platform, together with his glazed cap, and plunged to the rescue, risking his own life to save his little friend, and throwing the child and himself out of the way of the moving car. They both landed face down in sharp, fresh gravel ballast with such force as to drive the particles into the flesh, so that, when rescued, their appearance was somewhat alarming.

Mackenzie, like most other station agents, spent his salary before he got it and was unable to show his gratitude in the usual way. Instead, he offered to teach Edison telegraphy. The boy came daily, cutting short his railway trip. Within a few weeks he was more proficient than Mackenzie himself.

COME HELL OR HIGH WATER

CLARE FRANCIS

Clare Francis was the first British woman to take part in the Observer Royal Western Single-handed Transatlantic Race. She succeeded in beating the French-held women's record by finishing the course in twenty-nine days and was also the first British competitor in a conventional boat to complete. She survived thirty-five foot waves, gales, fog and icebergs. These extracts give a taste of her gruelling voyage.

THE WIND WAS NUDGING BACK towards the south-west again and increasing. It had all the looks of another wet interlude and by afternoon it was, as I struggled on the foredeck to raise the working jib and take another reef in the main. I resigned myself to another blow but was delighted to find that the wind suddenly backed and moderated. This was a nice surprise and I contemplated putting up more sail, but didn't rush into it because a sail change on the *Golly* still laid me out for half an hour. The wind kept dropping, though, and eventually I had to put up a larger jib or watch the *Golly* wallowing in the swell.

No sooner was the sail up and pulling, than the wind changed direction and increased again, so that once again I had too much sail up. Bother it, I thought, I'll leave it up and never mind! Immediately, a large black cloud came along with a squall underneath it and I was forced to shorten sail or have the boat sitting on her side. After another half hour the cloud passed and the wind dropped again. I could see it was going to be one of those nights. A weather forecast would be useful but, now that I was out of range of Radio 2 and the BBC shipping forecasts, it would have to come from elsewhere. Just before the start we had all been handed a brochure on the BBC Overseas Service together with a note saying that a special race forecast would be transmitted at 0330 GMT every day. This was ideal, and I looked for the required frequency on the Brookes and Gatehouse receiver. After a few minutes and with a great feeling of disappointment, I decided I didn't have it. Of course it was staring me in the face but, with my brain in slow gear, I kept looking at the wrong set of radio bands.

Still, no forecast could have told me that the wind would twist and turn, blow and then moderate throughout the night. At three in the morning I found myself lying panting in the cockpit having just changed down yet again, only to find the wind moderating once more. There was good seamanship and ridiculous keenness; I decided it was good seamanship to leave her undercanvased and ridiculous keenness to put up more sail again. I didn't have the strength to be keen anyway, and I staggered below to rest my shaking limbs. Soon I was able to congratulate myself on my foresight because another rain squall hit the boat and she was no longer undercanvased. After an hour's dozing I thought that I had really been very clever, because the squall was still blowing. About an hour later it began to occur to me that this was the longest squall I had ever experienced and, despite a very strong desire to roll over, block my ears and go to sleep, I pulled myself up and had a look outside. By that time the gale was well established and I found the *Golly* to be overpowered yet again. With a mental groan I staggered up on deck to pull down the flapping jib, to receive the

compulsory shot of water down the neck, and to get
another smaller jib onto the forestay. As soon as I had
winched the sail in, a strong blast of wind hit my cheek
and I noticed with interest that the anemometer read well
over 40 knots of wind. Another blast and I went back on
deck to lower everything, managing, yet again, to wrap
the main halyard around the radar reflector. This time I
wasn't going to waste all that effort by trying to free it and
I waited patiently for the action of the mast to whip it
clear. No good watching it, of course, it would never free
itself, so I slipped back to the cockpit and looked the other
way. After several secretive glances I gave up the subtle
approach and charged at the halyard, preparing myself to
flick and jerk at it for hours. I gave a first almighty heave,
prepared for a massive jerk, and looked up to see the
halyard swinging free as a bird.

The gale finally settled in from the south and it was
possible to make slow progress west under storm jib and
treble reefed main. If the first gale was unpleasant, this
one was appalling. Not only was I feeling unprepared for
another blow so soon after the first, but I was already
exhausted from the sail changing throughout the night.

And, needless to add, I was soaking wet. But at least I could do something about my wet clothes and, full of anticipation, I went below to search out some dry ones. It was an impossible job. Everytime I put my hand into a locker it came out wet and, as I discovered more and more dripping garments, my heart sank further and further. I could put up with a lot of discomfort for a short time but the prospect of being wet for another three weeks was almost impossible to contemplate. Out of piles of wet jeans, soaking sweaters and clammy socks I salvaged one suit of polar underwear and a jersey. These I carefully hung on the clothes line over the stove where I defied a tidal wave to reach them. From my position in the bunk, I watched over them with loving care. One day when all the world was dry, I would put on those wonderful clothes and feel that life was approximately a hundred times better.

The lockers had become wet from bilge water which was flung up the sides of the boat as the *Golly* jerked and gyrated over the waves. But the bilge itself was being filled with water from the toerail, the mast and various leaks of uncertain origin in the deck. The toerail had soaked nearly all my books and had wet most of the food stowed in the galley. Half my store of bread had got damp and I could almost see the mildew growing before my eyes. All the towels were dripping and I didn't dare look in the locker where the loo paper was kept. The leak above the radio was in full flood but I managed to catch a lot of it by balancing a cooking pot in a strategic position underneath. All I had to do was to remember to empty it every fifteen minutes before it got too full and the contents were shot across the cabin by a sudden movement of the boat.

And the movements of the boat were severe. She would rush at a wave, leap off the top and then crash down onto the other side, give a quick roll or flip, then rush at another. Sometimes she found nothing but air as she leapt off a crest and there would be a ghastly moment of silence before a terrible juddering crash as the bows hit water again. At times like that it was easy to imagine that the mast had just broken or the hull split in two, for it seemed impossible that any boat could take such a beating. But with the *Golly* it was all or nothing and I could not slow her down without stopping her altogether. So I left her as she was, water streaming over the decks, (and into the lockers) and her motion as wild as a washing machine's. Like a dirty dishcloth I was spun, rinsed and tumbled about until I should have been whiter than white. I tried wedging myself in my bunk but nearly got thrown out, so I tied myself in and lay there in a state of mental paralysis, allowing no thoughts to enter my mind. I heard a banging and crashing sound above the racket of the gale, but was too tired to go and investigate, choosing to watch the water spurting out from beside the mast instead. Even if I had known that the loo had broken loose and was committing hari-kari by painful degrees I wouldn't have minded much; my memories of it were not exactly pleasant. But then another noise came to my bleary attention and this one could not be ignored. Something was hitting against the hull and even before I looked I know what it would be. I had tied a sail down along the deck and, sure enough, the weight of water had pulled it free so that most of it was trailing in the sea. Five minutes later I had the sail below and another boot full of water. If life was bleak then it was bleaker three hours later. I allowed myself to become excited at the sight of a clear sky ahead and, quite certain the wind would drop, waited expectantly. The sun came out, the clouds disappeared, and then, to my dismay, the wind blew as strongly as ever, if not stronger.

So this was the great adventure, I thought disconsolately. Gales that went on for ever, wet long johns, soggy food that was impossible to cook, damp books that fell apart in your hands and, worst of all, no one to complain to. Of course there was a bright side; The *Golly* was managing herself very well and was giving me no cause for concern. Also, lit by the bright sunshine, the wind-swept sea did look magnificent as the great waves rolled across it in endless procession; it was just a pity we had to soldier through them. And there was the knowledge that the gale had to end sometime, although as the hours went by I couldn't help feeling a nagging doubt. There just had to be some gentle breezes and calm seas ahead. Then I would be able to sleep again, and eat again and, above all, be dry again, although I had some doubts about that too.

Gales go on for ever and then miraculously they end. At three the next morning the wind had dropped enough for me to put up more sail, breathe a sigh of relief and, together with my hot water bottle, snuggle up in a bunk and get some sleep.

I woke up feeling as though I had just come through a bout with Muhammed Ali; covered in bruises, woolly in the head and stiff all over. Changing sail seemed to take even longer than usual and I felt as weak as a kitten. "Must eat," I declared and made myself some porridge, which was no mean feat because the *Golly* was still at an impossible angle. Strangely, the wind had not died away or veered as it usually did after a gale. Instead it was a steady Force 5 or 6 from the west and the boat was hard on the wind, pushing through a lumpy sea. But I didn't even begin to think of what the weather might be planning and concentrated on getting some porridge down instead. I managed half of it, which was quite good, but I wished I could eat more. My weakness seemed to be worse and after the slightest exertion I had to sit down and rest. Mother would have been horrified and I only wished she were here to cook something I had an appetite for.

As I approached the Grand Banks it became bitterly cold.

It was as if the wind had blown out of an enormous refrigerator, and I could almost feel the arctic ice in its breath. There was a different smell in the air too, a strong scent of fish and decaying sea life, carried down with the melting ice.

And, as always, there was fog. Sometimes it would fade a little, but then it would swoop down as thick as ever, and we would be sailing into a white curtain again. I tried not to peer ahead too often because all I could see were the hundreds of icebergs my eyes conjured up and my nerves couldn't stand the strain.

The place had a terrible emptiness to it, a desolation that entered one's bones with every blast of icy wind. I had a strong impression of space and distance and for once I was aware of how very far from land we were. Normally I never thought beyond the three miles of water I could see around me, a miniature world across which the *Golly* seemed to be sailing for ever. But here, I was aware of what I was – a small person in the middle of a large ocean. And it was a cold and lonely feeling.

Loneliness was not something I often experienced at sea. I missed people, which is an entirely different thing, for it holds the promise of reunion and renewed companionship in the future. Also, the boat and the sea themselves were familiar old friends and, until either gave me cause to believe otherwise, I felt safe in their company. I have only ever felt real loneliness in big cities or other places where there are plenty of people about but no one to talk to. Normally I dislike being alone and if there are people around I will always seek them out. But here there was not much chance of finding someone to talk to so I didn't feel I was missing anything. It was the difference between going for a walk on your own with the prospect of seeing the family for tea and coming home to a silent and empty house to find a note stuck on the door: "Gone to a party – you're invited too!" but no indication as to where the party might be.

Out here in the deathly quiet and dank fog, I suddenly

wanted to be where I was sure everyone else must be: in the warm and sunny ocean to the south. For a moment I even imagined I had been sucked hundreds of miles to the north, and it was only by frequent looks at the compass and chart that I convinced myself I was indeed heading south of Newfoundland.

The best remedy for loneliness and thoughts of the Arctic was to keep myself occupied, but even when busy down in the cabin, I felt an eerie atmosphere that made me shiver. Not that I wasn't shivering anyway. However many clothes I put on, I was still cold. I must have looked like an overweight teddy bear, and I certainly felt it as I rolled around the boat, bouncing off the bulkheads. I wore so many layers that my arms stuck out from my sides as if my deodorant had turned to concrete. On top of a vest and paper panties I wore Mother's thermo-nuclear underwear consisting of silky long johns and top, then a polar suit made of thick tufted wool, and finally a pair of old jeans and two very baggy sweaters. On my head I wore a wool balaclava and around my neck a towel. When going on deck I would put oilskins on top of all this, although it was a tremendous effort to haul them on and resulted in much puffing and panting. However, after I had been sail changing or winching for a while I would regret nearly every layer of clothing. Within minutes I would be dying of heat, and inside my super-efficient oilskins it felt like the hothouse at Kew; very warm, very humid and very uncomfortable.

But while my body was burning hot, my hands were freezing. The one thing I had forgotten was gloves. Not that I could have worn them to handle the ropes, but it would have been nice to keep my hands warm between sail changes so that they wouldn't freeze so quickly on deck. My fingers were already cracked and swollen from heaving on sails and ropes, and now that they were cold as well it was all I could do to grasp a halyard.

Once, as I was sitting on deck sucking and blowing on my fingers, waiting for them to thaw out and allow me to finish a sail change, it occurred to me that I was either on the wrong route or mad. It was mid-summer and if I were only a few miles to the south I could be lying under a burning hot sun, frying my skin to a crisp frazzle and sipping a gin on the afterdeck. Instead, here I was, doing my best to impersonate a polar bear, not only in appearance but in habitat.

What was more, I was tired and fed up. After seventeen days of sail-grappling, and being thrown around, and not getting any sleep I suddenly decided that I was very tired indeed and didn't feel prepared to face another of those killing sail changes. Far from getting more practised at dropping the genoas neatly, I seemed to throw them over the side all the time. And sitting on the lowered sail didn't appear to impress the wind any more; it would blow into a fold of the canvas and form a balloon that grew and grew until the sail billowed up into a small spinnaker. When I jumped on it or grabbed at it or lay on it, the balloon would only reappear elsewhere. After much grappling I would eventually persuade the sail to bunch itself up and disappear down the forehatch, only to face the same kind of undisciplined behaviour from the next sail when I pulled that up on deck. There was one sail, the Number One Genoa, which was particularly heavy and unbending and it took me all my strength to move it about. I didn't bother to bag that sail because I could never have lifted it up in one piece. Instead I left it loose in the sailbin so that I could pull it up section by section. With hands that would hardly grip, this task was a real struggle.

Neither was sail hoisting and winching any easier than it had been when I was afflicted by the Lurgy. My hands complained bitterly at contact with the ropes and I didn't seem to have the energy to wind on the winches. I had always winched in the large genoas in easy stages; getting some sail in, then resting, pulling a little more and another pause, and then, if the last few inches were impossible, I would head the *Golly* into the wind to take the pressure off the sail and quickly winch in the rest. But now it wasn't weakness that made it hard, it was a deep tiredness and, I had to admit, a general lack of enthusiasm.

When the wind dropped to a light breeze, it was necessary to replace the wind vane on the self-steering with a larger, lighter one to prevent the gear from becoming sluggish. Changing vanes normally took me a moment but now my cold hands fumbled and failed to grip and suddenly the light vane was over the side and floating in the wake. I knew I could go back for it and, as I kept telling myself, I really *should*. And yet, as I watched it disappearing fast behind, I knew I wouldn't be turning the boat around. There was something repugnant about turning back the way I had come, even for a few minutes, and as the vane disappeared into the fog I was rather relieved that I had left it too late. It was always unnerving to lose something over the side, not necessarily because it was a thing of value, but because it was a reminder of how quickly it could happen to a person – meaning oneself – and how irredeemable such an accident would be. From time to time I would throw an empty tin over the side and watch it vanishing behind, just to remind me to hold on tight when working on the foredeck.

In the dense fog and cold, I stayed below as much as possible, huddling around the heater like a road mender at his brazier. I would thaw my hands, then swivel around to scorch my feet and socks until they had stopped steaming. But I did not like to leave the heater on when I was asleep and unable to watch it, so I relied on two sleeping bags and my faithful hot water bottle to keep me warm at night. Even so, I always felt cold, mainly as a result of my hourly excursions on deck. My body clock seemed to turn off my interior heating system at night and I shivered violently as soon as I got up. By the time I returned to my bunk, my teeth were rattling like castanets and I was shaking to the rhythm of a fast rumba. It took several minutes to warm up again and fall asleep.

As I awoke I became aware that something was wrong. The boat was moving wildly, rolling from side to side then suddenly lurching over and staying there, shuddering with strain. With a groan I remembered the spinnaker. By the feel of the boat, it should have been down hours ago. Still dazed and heavy-eyed, I could not think how long I had been asleep, but it must have been well over an hour, probably nearer two. I pulled on my boots and oilskins and staggered up on deck, nervous of what I might find.

It could have been worse. The wind was Force 5 and still from the east. The seas were not any larger than I would have expected, but they were sufficient to make the boat roll considerably and slew from side to side. It was impossible for the self-steering to anticipate these yaws until too late, and only when the boat was well off track could the wind vane sense it and pull her back. But the pull of the spinnaker was often too powerful and *Golly* would continue to veer off until the spinnaker held her over on her side, lee rail under and main boom dragging in the water. These broaches were horrible to see. They put a lot of strain on the boat, particularly the mast and rigging, and I hurried to lower the spinnaker before she broached again.

Lowering a spinnaker in a strong breeze when alone at night is a frightening experience. One mistake and the spinnaker can tear and wrap itself round the forestay, making it impossible to raise a foresail again. The spinnaker boom, the guy and sheet are all under enormous strain and one slip can result in serious breakage. I wasn't going to take any chances and approached the task with caution. Better to be slow and sure than make a mistake.

The "Salami" would not slide down over a full spinnaker, so I had to half-collapse the sail before attempting to pull the sausage down over it. Having eased the sheet, there was a terrible commotion of flapping canvas and rattling gear as I rushed forward to pull the sleeve down. I tugged on the line, but nothing happened. I pulled harder, but the mouth of the "Salami" stayed obstinately where it was, at the top of the sail. Just then the *Golly* broached and I had to cling on as she dived round on her side. For a moment all was confusion, then she righted herself and thundered off into the night. I yanked on the line again, but I could make no impression on the "Salami" at all. A fine time to jam itself! I tried collapsing the spinnaker further but after a terrifying broach I decided that, whatever the method, the important thing was to get the spinnaker down quickly.

The traditional method of lowering a spinnaker is most satisfactory if you have a crew of five or ten, but single-handed it requires five arms and, by my method, three feet. Having let one corner of the sail fly, you pull on the other corner, gather in the foot of the sail (quite impossible), then with your arms full of sail you let off the halyard (this was where the feet came in – I wrapped them round the sail in place of arms). The halyard must then be lowered slowly (this was where the third foot was needed – I put the halyard under my foot, let it run out a way, then stopped it by stamping hard. Except I sometimes missed, or found my leg in the air with the halyard wrapped round my foot and pulling hard). As the sail comes down, all is meant to be gathered in tidily, and in no time the spinnaker should be lying at one's feet in a neat pile.

This time I dropped half the thing in the water, and twice nearly took off behind the ballooning sail. Still, it was down, and I breathed a sigh of relief. Half an hour later I had sorted out the mess of lines, booms, guys and sheets, and hoisted a jib boomed out to windward.

Sleep. I felt that was all and everything I had ever wanted, and I shot below to fall into a heavy and dreamless slumber.

I heard the pinger an hour later and dutifully crawled out of my bunk. The wind had increased, and the boat was running too fast again so that I lowered the jib and left her

under mainsail only. This was lazy of me. I should have reefed the main and put up a smaller jib, but I couldn't face the effort and hurried back to my bunk instead.

At three in the morning (everything at sea happens at three in the morning), I awoke with that familiar feeling that something was wrong again. I was thick with sleep and longing to snuggle into the depths of my sleeping bag, but I managed to pull myself up and take a look on deck. I was shocked to find it was blowing a gale and the boat was careering downhill, veering from side to side as the large waves caught her from behind. Then I did something extraordinary. I must have been half asleep with my brain even more addled than usual. Nothing else could explain the stupidity of my actions.

I decided I must reef the main immediately. Usually, even in the worst crises, I can astonish myself by taking a calm look at the situation and setting about everything in a careful way. But this time I rushed into action, without thought and without consideration of the consequences. I decided I must get the *Golly* up into the wind to reef the main, and straight away. Mustn't strain the self-steering, I thought; mustn't use it to bring her up. . . it'll be too sudden for it.

This was completely backwards thinking. I knew very well that the self-steering was all right as long as it was in use, but that once it was disconnected it was free to swing too far and destroy itself. But somehow my brain had decided that the exact opposite was true and was determined to unlatch the gear.

Perhaps it was also fear from the terrible rushing downhill, that violent swerving from side to side that made me panic. It was unnerving to be rocketing into the darkness, more or less out of control. Anyway, whatever it was, tiredness or fear, I did it. I unlatched the gear and pushed the tiller hard over so that the *Golly* would shoot up into the wind and allow me to reef. As the boat turned, the self-steering was thrust sideways. Then, as she fell back again, the gear was pushed the other way. Instinctively I looked back at the gear and my heart froze. All four of the metal struts were bent out of recognition.

The full idiocy of what I had done dawned on me like a blow from a sledge hammer. It was such an obvious and basic mistake – and so irredeemable. I groaned and muttered "Oh, you twit!" – which was quite kind under the circumstances – and drew a mental breath.

It was difficult to decide how serious my situation really was. One moment I would look at the twisted arms and despair, and the next I would feel a sudden hope that I could once again repair them. The implications of failure were unpleasant – a long trek up to Nova Scotia without self-steering – so I knew I must at least try to straighten those arms. I lowered the mainsail and had a close look at the gear. It would be impossibly difficult to mend the gear in position, so I decided I would have to bring the lower section of the gear inboard where I could dismantle it with greater ease. The only problem was the weight and size of the gear. Made of a heavy alloy, and over five feet in height, it weighed about ten stone to my seven.

Gathering the necessary tools around me, I started on the long and tedious task. I disconnected the various ropes and lines attached to the gear, leaving one line firmly secured to both the gear and the boat. Even allowing for my depleted brain power, I could see it wouldn't be a good idea to drop the gear over the side. Next I had to slide the main spindle out. The whole of the lower moving section of the gear swung on this main spindle, a stainless steel rod an inch thick. Once it was removed the section would be completely unsupported and would drop into the water, whereupon I would pull it up over the rail, hopefully. But I found the removal of the spindle was not just a matter of sliding it out. The gear had to be held up in position while I worked the spindle out, inch by inch. As before I was leaning over the stern rail, gripping with my feet, and often up to my elbows in water. But now I was trying to hold a weight in a precise position while tugging at a spindle as well.

Finally, after much effort, the spindle came away and I felt the lower section of the gear fall as I tried to take its weight. I held on grimly, resting a moment while I waited for a suitable wave that would help me swing the gear round and up over the rail. Without the buoyancy of the water I could never have swung the gear, let alone held it. At last I felt the stern rising and saw the surface rushing up as a large wave approached. I swung the gear round and heaved.

I didn't quite make it first time and, with a gasp, I had to let the gear fall into the water again. By this time my arms were very tired and I had to take a long rest before attempting the lift again. I hung there over the stern, holding firmly onto that precious metal, and waited for perhaps half a minute. A large wave came, I heaved, and got the gear half-way onto the rail. But the weight was still on the wrong side and I felt it slipping back. Summoning

some strength I gave a last pull and managed to slide it over another inch. At last, by swinging my weight on it, the gear pivoted over onto my side of the rail. Then, after a final heave, it fell on top of me. I lay back on the west deck, exhausted but very relieved.

I lay there for five minutes or so, enjoying the rest. I was not in any hurry to get on with the repairs. They would take a long time at whatever speed I tackled them, so I might as well take them slowly and thoughtfully – unlike my earlier actions. Every moment that the *Golly* lay there drifting, we were forfeiting marvellous mileage. Seven or eight knots was the *Golly's* speed downwind in a good breeze. It was sad to lose such easy progress, but it was more important to get the gear repaired properly than to rush the job and bend the gear again.

Leaving the *Golly* drifting, I dismantled the bent struts and took them below for that favourite task of mine: weld-bending as I called it. After heating the struts I attempted to bend them. But either the blow lamp and the gas rings never got the struts hot enough or else the metal wasn't heatable anyway, because the heat never seemed to make much difference. So in the end it was always back to plain old bending. The main problem was finding some leverage against which to bend the metal. Most of the interior fittings were wood and too soft to form a good base for the vice, so that the boat echoed to the sound of splintering wood as I tried the vice on bulkheads, bunk ends and shelf edges. By the time I had got the worst bends out, the boat looked like matchwood.

It took me five hours of sweat and toil to straighten the struts and even then they looked like snakes. As before, I hung on them, swung on them, heaved, pushed and yanked. Sometimes I would even make the kinks worse by exerting the pressure in the wrong place but I only did that five times, then I learnt. Quick, I am.

I also discovered that I was brainless, for the tenth time that day. As I grunted and pulled and heaved I suddenly realized that I had wasted five whole hours in useless pursuit, trying to bend metal against wood. There had been the perfect leverage available all the time – I had been so intent on using the vice that I had forgotten it would be completely unnecessary if I levered the metal directly against the most solid and well-bedded metal you could find. The engine. It took me ten minutes to straighten all four struts against the engine, and the thought of five hours' wasted effort almost made me laugh or weep, I wasn't sure which. I knocked my head against a locker a couple of times, but didn't want any more splintered wood around, so I gave up self-reproach and crawled back on deck to reassemble the gear.

ANTARCTIC CHRISTMAS

CAPTAIN ROBERT F. SCOTT

from The Voyage of the 'Discovery'

Robert Falcon Scott was an English polar explorer who died during a famous expedition to the South Pole in 1912. He and four other men arrived at the pole on 17 January only to find that the Norwegian, Roald Amundsen, had arrived a month earlier. On the return journey, all five Englishmen perished. Scott's diary, recording an earlier Antarctic expedition in 1902, vividly illustrates the day to day conditions the explorers endured.

DECEMBER 24TH — Wilson examined us again this morning. I asked him quietly the result, and he said, "A little more." It is trying, but we both agree that it is not time yet to say "Turn." But we have one fact to comfort us tonight – we have passed on to a much harder surface, and though it still holds a layer of an inch or two of feathery snow, beneath that it is comparatively firm, and we are encamped on quite a hard spot. If the dogs have not improved, they have not grown much worse during the past day or two; their relative strength alters a good deal, as the following tale will show: "Stripes" and "Gus" pull next one another; a week ago one had great difficulty in preventing "Stripes" from leaping across and seizing "Gus's" food. He was very cunning about it; he waited till one's back was turned, and

then was over and back in a moment. Time has its revenges: now "Gus" is the stronger, and tonight he leapt across and seized "Stripes's" choicest morsel. At other times they are not bad friends these two; loser and winner seem to regard this sort of thing as part of the game. After all, it is but "the good old rule, the simple plan," but of course we right matters when we detect such thefts.

Tonight is Christmas Eve. We have been thinking and talking about the folk at home, and also much about our plans for tomorrow.

December 25th, Christmas Day — ... For a week we have looked forward to this day with childish delight, and, long before that, we decided that it would be a crime to go to bed hungry on Christmas night; so the week went in planning a gorgeous feed. Each meal and each item of each meal we discussed and rediscussed. The breakfast was to be a glorious spread; the Primus was to be kept going ten or even fifteen minutes longer than usual. Lunch for once was to be warm and comforting; and supper! – well,

154

supper was to be what supper has been.

In fact, we meant this to be a wonderful day, and everything has conspired to make it so.

When we awoke to wish each other "A merry Christmas" the sun was shining warmly through our green canvas roof. We were outside in a twinkling, to find the sky gloriously clear and bright, with not a single cloud in its vast arch. Away to the westward stretched the long line of gleaming coastline; the sunlight danced and sparkled in the snow beneath our feet, and not a breath of wind disturbed the serenity of the scene. It was a glorious morning, but we did not stay to contemplate it, for we had even more interesting facts to occupy us, and were soon inside the tent sniffing at the savoury steam of the cooking-pot. Then breakfast was ready and before each of us lay a whole pannikin-full of biscuit and seal-liver, fried in bacon and pemmican fat. It was gone in no time, but this and a large spoonful of jam to follow left a sense of comfort which we had not experienced for weeks, and we started to pack up in a frame of mind that was wholly joyful.

After this we started on the march, and felt at once the improvement of surface that came to us last night; so great was it that we found we three alone could draw the sledges, and for once the driver was silent and the whip but rarely applied. The dogs merely walked along with slack traces, and we did not attempt to get more out of them. No doubt an outsider would have thought our procession funereal enough, but to us the relief was inexpressible; and so we trudged on from 11.30 to 4 p.m., when we thoroughly enjoyed our lunch, which consisted of hot cocoa and plasmon with a whole biscuit and another spoonful of jam. We were off again at 5.30, and marched on till 8.30, when we camped in warmth and comfort and with the additional satisfaction of having covered nearly eleven miles, the longest march we have made for a long time.

Then we laid ourselves out for supper, reckless of consequences, having first had a Christmas wash and brush-up. Redolent of soap, we sat around the cooking-pot, whilst into its boiling contents was poured a double "whack" of everything. In the *hoosh* that followed one could stand one's spoon with ease, and still the Primus hissed on, as once again our cocoa was brought to the boiling-point. Meanwhile I had observed Shackleton ferreting about in his bundle, out of which he presently produced a spare sock, and stowed away in the toe of that sock was a small round object about the size of a cricket ball, which when brought to light, proved to be a noble "plum-pudding." Another dive into his lucky-bag and out came a crumpled piece of artificial holly. Heated in the cocoa, our plum-pudding was soon steaming hot, and stood on the cooker-lid crowned with its decoration. For once we divided food without "shut-eye."

I am writing over my second pipe. The sun is still slowly circling our small tent in a cloudless sky, the air is warm

and quiet, all is pleasant without, and within we have a sense of comfort we have not known for many a day; we shall sleep well tonight – no dreams, no tightening of the belt.

We have been chattering away gaily, and not once has the conversation turned to food. We have been wondering what Christmas is like in England – possibly very damp, gloomy, and unpleasant, we think; we have been wondering, too, how our friends picture us. They will guess that we are away on our sledge journey, and will perhaps think of us on plains of snow; but few, I think, will imagine the truth, that for us this has been the reddest of all red-letter days.

December 26th — ... Poor Wilson has had an attack of snow-blindness, in comparison with which our former attacks may be considered as nothing; we were forced to camp early on account of it, and during the whole afternoon he has been writhing in horrible agony. It is distressing enough to see, knowing that one can do nothing to help. Cocaine has only a very temporary effect, and in the end seems to make matters worse. I have never seen an eye so terribly bloodshot and inflamed as that which is causing the trouble, and the inflammation has spread to the eyelid. He describes the worst part as an almost intolerable stabbing and burning of the eyeball; it is the nearest approach to illness we have had, and one can only hope that it is not going to remain serious.

Shackleton did butcher tonight, and "Brownie" was victim. Poor little dog! His life has been very careworn of late, and it is probably a happy release.

December 27th — Late last night Wilson got some sleep, and this morning he was better; all day he has been pulling alongside the sledges with his eyes comletely covered. It is tiresome enough to see our snowy world through the slit of a goggle, but to march blindfolded with an empty stomach for long hours touches a pitch of monotony which I shall be glad to avoid. We covered a good ten miles today by sledge-meter, though I think that instrument is clogging and showing short measure. The dogs have done little, but they have all walked, except "Stripes," who broke down and had to be carried on the sledge; he was quite limp when I picked him up, and his thick coat poorly hides the fact that he is nothing but skin and bone. Yesterday I noticed that we were approaching what appeared to be a deeper bay than usual, and this afternoon this opening developed in the most interesting manner.

On the near side is a bold, rocky, snow-covered cape, and all day we have been drawing abreast of this; as we rapidly altered its bearing this afternoon it seemed to roll back like some vast sliding gate, and gradually there stood revealed one of the most glorious mountain scenes we have yet witnessed. Walking opposite to Wilson I was trying to keep him posted with regard to the changes, and I think my reports of this part must have sounded curious. It was with some excitement I noticed that new mountain ridges were appearing as high as anything we had seen to the north, but, to my surprise, as we advanced the ridges grew still higher, as no doubt did my tones. Then, instead of a downward turn in the distant outline came a steep upward line; Pelion was heaped on Ossa, and it can be imagined that we pressed the pace to see what would happen next, till the end came in a gloriously sharp double peak crowned with a few flecks of cirrus cloud.

We can no longer call this opening a bay; it runs for many miles in to the foot of the great range, and is more in the nature of an inlet. But all our thoughts in camp tonight turn to this splendid twin-peaked mountain, which, even in such a lofty country, seems as a giant among pigmies. We all agree that from Sabine to the south the grandest eminences cannot compare in dignity with this monster. We have decided that at last we have found something which is fitting to bear the name of him whom we must always the most delight to honour, and "Mount Markham" it shall be called in memory of the father of the expedition.

THE MYSTERIOUS RAYS

ANGELA BULL

from Marie Curie

Polish-born Marie Curie (1867-1934) and her French husband Pierre worked together to discover the radioactive elements radium and polonium. In 1902 they managed to extract one gram of these substances from over eight tons of pitch-blende. The Curies shared the 1903 Nobel Prize with Becquerel (the discoverer of radioactivity). After Pierre's death in 1906, Marie succeeded in completely isolating radium and was awarded a second Nobel Prize in 1911. This extract shows how hard Marie and Pierre worked to make their discoveries.

THE CURIES RENTED a three-roomed flat. There was not much furniture because Marie hated dusting, and the meals were terrible. She found boiling a pan of beans far more difficult than any scientific experiment. But food and possessions were not important to Marie and Pierre. Their real life was in the laboratory. Pierre continued his research on magnetism; Marie published the results of her research on steel. They were very happy, and when their first daughter, Irene, was born in 1897, Marie thankfully left the care of her to Pierre's father, who had come to live with them.

She had decided to work for the advanced degree of Doctor of Science, and by 1897 she was looking for a new subject to research. Very recently a scientist called Henri Becquerel had discovered that uranium salts spontaneously gave off rays of an unknown nature. The mystery of the rays fascinated Marie. What caused them? What could they do? With Pierre's encouragement, she chose the uranium rays for her research subject.

Because the Sorbonne could not offer her any room, she started her work in an unused laboratory at Pierre's School of Physics and Chemistry. It would have been hard to find anywhere less suitable for important scientific research. The tiny, badly-equipped laboratory was bakingly hot in summer, and in winter cold and damp enough to interfere with her precision instruments. But after her attic years, unfavourable conditions did not worry Marie, and she plunged excitedly into her experiments.

She soon discovered that the rays given off by uranium were very unusual. She examined them in conditions of heat, light, wetness and darkness, and nothing seemed to affect them. She compared other elements with uranium, and found that only one, thorium, gave out similar rays, and was thus – to use the term she invented – radioactive.

As her experiments continued, it began to seem that some minerals containing uranium were more radioactive than she would have expected. Could they include another, as yet unidentified, element, more strongly radioactive than uranium? When Marie mentioned this theory to other physicists, they refused to believe her. Scornfully they told her that all the scientific elements were known already. Was it likely that a woman – a woman! – had found a new one? But Marie would not change her mind. She knew what she had proved in her odd little laboratory; and in April 1898 she announced, in a scientific magazine, that pitch-blende – a mineral which included uranium – certainly also contained a powerfully radioactive, and previously undiscovered, element.

She now had to prove her theory by isolating the new element. It was a daunting task, but Marie was no longer working alone. Pierre, who had followed her experiments with enormous interest, abandoned his own research to help her. They worked side by side, jotting down their observations in the same notebook. By chemical means they analysed the pitch-blende, and found to their surprise that it contained *two* new elements – one which Marie called polonium, in honour of Poland, and another, stronger element, extraordinarily radioactive, which they called radium.

The other scientists remained doubtful. The elements isolated by the Curies were in such minute traces they could barely be said to exist at all. Marie and Pierre knew they must produce them in large enough quantities to overcome disbelief. To do this they would need to acquire and treat a considerable mass of pitch-blende.

A genius is said to be a person with an infinite capacity for taking pains. If the definition is correct, Marie showed herself to be a genius now. She was determined to prove, beyond a shadow of doubt, the existence of radium, and she did not mind how long or how hard she had to work to do so. Searching for a cheap source of pitch-blende, because they had very little money, she remembered that it was mined in the pine forests of Austria, and the uranium taken out for making glass. The waste pitch-blende, left after the uranium had been extracted, could be just what she needed; and with the help of an Austrian colleague, she managed to get a tonne, free of charge.

Sacks of it arrived one day at the laboratory on a coal wagon, a dusty brown mineral mixed with pine needles from the forest where it had been mined. There was far too much for the laboratory to hold. But across the yard was a little wooden shed, even more primitive than the laboratory, and here the gigantic task was begun.

"It was in that miserable old shed," Marie wrote, "that the best and happiest days of our life were spent, entirely consecrated to work."

Outside in the yard, with a cauldron slung over a fire, Marie smelted down the pitch-blende, twenty kilograms at a time. She worked in a dirty, acid-stained overall, stirring the boiling mass with an iron rod. In the shed Pierre analysed the mineral extracts she obtained. They talked endlessly about the wonderful, powerful element they would isolate.

"What will it be like?" Marie asked: and Pierre answered, "I should like it to have a very beautiful colour."

Month after month the work went on. When the smelting was at last finished, Marie joined Pierre at his analysis in the shed. Its old wooden tables were loaded with more and more concentrated solutions of radium. But as, enthralled, they studied their new element, they failed to realize a most important thing. Its mysterious rays were extremely harmful to human beings.

Handling it constantly, breathing in its gas, Marie and Pierre began to suffer from its secret effects. Marie's

fingers were painfully burned. Pierre ached all over, as if
he had rheumatism. They were tired. They took a long
time to recover from minor coughs and colds. Yet they
never connected their ailments with radioactivity. For
years they had been indifferent to their own comfort, and
they were still the same. They seldom took a break. They
gulped down inadequate meals so as not to waste time,
not caring how thin they became. Often they ate in the
shed, unaware that the radium-laden atmosphere was
contaminating even their sandwiches.

Sometimes, when they had finished work and gone
home, the fascination of the radium would draw them
back. They had been working on it for four years, and the
new element was in its most concentrated form, when, just
before bedtime one night, Marie suggested to Pierre a last
visit to the shed. They hurried through the dim Paris
streets, and Pierre put his key into the shed door.

"Don't light the lamp for a minute," whispered Marie. "Do you remember how you wished that radium was a beautiful colour?"

As the door swung back, they saw that Pierre's wish had come true. All round the shed the glass tubes of radium shone through the darkness, with a strange, blue, phosphorescent glow.

"Working in a shed might sound romantic," Marie wrote, long after the discovery of radium had made her famous, "but the romantic element was not an advantage. It wore out our strength, and delayed our accomplishment."

The poor conditions in the shed put extra stress on two people already weakened by exposure to radiation. It was always cold, the floor was trodden earth, plaster flaked from the ceiling, the tap dripped. Only scientists as utterly dedicated as Marie and Pierre could have persevered with their research in such surroundings; and they were human enough to feel resentment at times and long for a better laboratory.

If only, Marie sometimes reflected sadly, Pierre's brilliance was recognized, he might be offered a new job, with access to a well-equipped laboratory. The Sorbonne should have made him a professor, but people who wanted academic posts were supposed to go humbly round their colleagues begging for support, and Pierre refused to do this. He knew that, with such a system, good positions went, not to those who deserved them, but to those who were best at currying favour. He wanted the university simply to acknowledge the value of his work, and this they did not do. The French government, in 1902, actually offered him their highest decoration, the Legion of Honour, for his contribution to French science, but Pierre turned it down. "I do not feel the slightest need of being decorated," he wrote, "but I am in the greatest need of a laboratory." Still the academic world ignored him.

The Curies were always short of money. Marie had no

salary or grant, and Pierre's salary was so low that it was quickly swallowed up by their living expenses, and by the wages of the maid and nurse, who looked after the house and little Irene. There was none to spare for advancing their research, and so, to earn a bit more, Marie took a job in a girls' school, where she taught physics two days a week. She was an excellent teacher, one of the first to allow her pupils to try practical experiments. More importantly, the work gave her a regular break from the contaminated atmosphere of the shed – something which Pierre never had. But Marie did not realize her good fortune. She only grumbled at the time she wasted in preparing her lessons, teaching, and travelling to and fro.

Still the research went on; still it was their supreme preoccupation. Between 1899 and 1904 Marie and Pierre published thirty-two articles about their work. Their discovery of a new, exciting element could no longer be doubted, and mounting interest in radioactivity spread throughout the scientific world. An elderly professor, who had followed their reports, was warned by his doctor that he had not long to live. "I can't die yet!" he exclaimed crossly. "I want to know more about radium."

Not only was radium gaining recognition as a vitally important new element by scientists in the new field of atomic physics. Ordinary people, who read simplified accounts of the discovery in their newspapers, were fascinated as well. The knowledge that their work was arousing such interest spurred the Curies on. Nothing but radium mattered. When a friend suggested that they might relax occasionally, and even eat a meal without talking about physics the whole time, Marie and Pierre took no notice.

In March 1902 they achieved their long-awaited goal. There in the shed, in a glass tube, were crystals of pure radium, made from the pitch-blende, and visible to human eyes for the first time. Radium looked like ordinary salt, but it was a million times more radioactive than uranium.

Marie and Pierre discovered that its rays penetrated every mineral except lead. For their own sake they should, from then on, have worked with the radium in lead containers, but that would have taken time and money which they could not spare. It was much easier and cheaper to go on using ordinary glass containers, even though their hands were often burned through the glass. They did not understand the seriousness of the burns. Pierre, indeed, burned his own arm deliberately, and recorded the developing stages of the injury with scientific detachment. It had certainly not occurred to them that everything in the shed, from the tables to the dust in the atmosphere, was becoming radioactive. Even now their notebooks are still too dangerous to be handled without precautions.

In 1903 Marie submitted an account of her work for her doctor's degree. She called it *Researches on Radioactive Substances* by Madame Sklodovska-Curie. The examiners summoned her, as was the custom, to appear in public, and be questioned about it.

The new black dress, which Bronya persuaded her to buy, was Marie's only concession to the drama of the occasion. It was right, she thought, to give a dry, factual description of her discoveries; and although an excited audience filled the hall, Marie took no notice of them, but sat facing the examiners, with her burned hands and untidy hair, explaining her work in the most matter-of-fact way, sometimes pausing to sketch a diagram on the blackboard. But her flat words could not quench the universal enthusiasm. She was awarded her degree, with the citation, "very honourable".

Before publishing her results, Marie had taken time to consider what she was doing. If she patented her technique for treating pitch-blende, other people who followed her method of producing radium would have to pay for the right to do so. The Curies could have become rich; rich enough to build a proper laboratory. Tempting though the idea was, Marie rejected it. To profit financially from a discovery was contrary to the disinterested scientific spirit in which she and Pierre had always tried to work.

But by now the Curies were winning recognition, and even fame. There were both genuine scientists and celebrity-hunters in the audience which attended a lecture given by Pierre at London's Royal Institute. As he pulled a glass tube of radium from his pocket, the New Zealand physicist, Ernest Rutherford, noticed the terrible marks on his hands. He noticed, too, that Pierre spilled a few grains – fifty years later the room was still so radioactive it needed decontaminating. Pierre noticed neither the tiny mishap, nor his own familiar burns. He was calculating how many laboratories could be bought with the jewellery worn by the ladies in the audience.

Six months later the Curies were awarded the Nobel Prize for Physics, one of the greatest honours in the scientific world. Suddenly, everyone was talking about them. Journalists besieged the shed, and mail arrived by the sackful, with letters of congratulation, requests for autographs, even poems praising radium. Pierre and Marie had no idea how to cope with the publicity. Although they knew their results would interest other scientists, they had never imagined such an outcry in the popular press, such a demand for interviews and photographs. They hated being hailed as superstars; that was not what science was about. They were dedicated to the advancement of knowledge, not the advancement of the Curies. When Marie was recognized in the street, she refused to admit her identity. More and more she and Pierre withdrew from the world, shutting themselves up amongst the still unsuspected dangers of their shed.

For it was dangerous. Neither Marie nor Pierre was well enough to go to Sweden to receive the prize. Pierre was particularly ill, with such pains in his body and limbs that for days he could only stay in bed.

Ironically, the burning of his arm had been part of an investigation into the biological effects of radium. Since it could destroy body cells, he began, with some medical friends, to consider if it could be used to treat cancer. The idea that radium could burn away diseased cells was greeted with enthusiasm. Experiments were tried with mice; and, in the last scientific paper he wrote, Pierre mentioned that a side effect of the radium on them was the destruction of their white blood corpuscles. It will never be known if Pierre thought of applying this chance discovery to human beings, especially to himself and Marie. Was he too tired and limp to inquire if radioactivity had been destroying *their* white corpuscles – the element in the blood that fights infection? Or did he guess the truth, and keep it to himself?

Life should have been improving for the Curies. Not only were they enriched by their prize money, but their ordinary income had soared. At last Pierre had been made a professor at the Sorbonne, with Marie appointed as his chief laboratory assistant. In their new laboratory they tackled the tough problem of measuring the emanation of radium. At home there was a new baby, Eva. But nothing could be properly enjoyed – not as those early days in the shed had been enjoyed. They were exhausted, and Pierre was depressed too. He had begun to have nightmare visions of what might happen if radium got into criminal hands. And could it somehow be used in warfare? He almost wished Marie had never discovered her new element.

Marie was very worried about him. He had changed from an eager scientist into a weary pessimist. He looked thin and ill. But if anything happened to him, how could she go on? She depended on him so much.

"Pierre," she said one day, "if one of us" (she meant him) "disappeared, the other could not survive."

For the last time Pierre roused himself to defend his old ideals.

"You are wrong," he answered. "Whatever happens, a scientist's work must go on."

THE THAMES TUNNEL

JOHN PUDNEY

from Brunel and his World

Isambard Kingdom Brunel (1806-1859) was one of the great engineers of the industrial revolution, a builder of ships, bridges, railways and tunnels. His father, Marc Isambard Brunel, was also a successful engineer. Young Isambard joined his father in his engineering practice, and helped him on one of his most ambitious schemes, a tunnel under the river Thames. This was never properly completed, but Isambard went on to become the greatest engineer of his day.

THE THAMES TUNNEL, the first beneath a navigable river, was twelve hundred feet long and took eighteen years and twenty-three days to build. Between 1825 and 1843 it was the scene of fearful hazards and adventures, and there were many casualties. Yet even when disaster threatened, or work had to cease altogether through lack of money, famous men and women from all walks of life and many nations were given VIP treatment at the workings. The public in their thousands paid to participate in one of the wonders of the age – to walk, even for a short distance, beneath the waters of the Thames. This string of visitors provided a small income to the impoverished promoters, even during the seven years when the unfinished tunnel was closed. *The Times* of course christened it "The Great Bore". It was the younger Brunel who carried the burden of the work and risked his life – and the lives of others – in hair-raising adventures below ground. Indeed, he grew up with the Tunnel.

There were many references to him in the father's journal. In 1825 for instance:

Isambard incessantly in the works, most actively employed, shows much intelligence. . . . Isambard was the greatest part of the night in the works. . . . Isambard was in the frames the whole night and day till dinner-hour. . . . Isambard the whole day until 2 at night. . . . Isambard has been every night and day too in the works. I relieved him at 3.

Two years later, when some three hundred feet of the Tunnel had been completed, young Isambard celebrated his twenty-first birthday with a party beneath the river. During that month of April 1827 the Tunnel workings, already internationally famous, were a source of public as well as private entertainment. "By way of calling public attention to the Tunnel", a concert was held and the acoustics were judged remarkably good. Marc Isambard particularly praised the quality of the clarinet. But with upwards of seven hundred visitors coming in every day he also expressed some anxiety.

"Notwithstanding every prudence on our part, a disaster may still occur. *May it not be when the arch is full of visitors*! It is too awful to think of it. I have done my part by recommending to the directors to shut the tunnel."

Two days later he noted: "The water increased very much at nine o'clock. This is very inquiétant! My apprehensions are not groundless. I apprehend nothing, however, as to the safety of the men, but first the visitors,

and next, a total invasion of the river. We must be prepared for the Worst." Even that degree of anxiety did not prevent him from doing the honours the following day.

"I attended Lady Raffles to the frames, most uneasy all the while as if I had a presentiment. . . ."

That same evening the river broke in while young Isambard, his assistant Gravatt and a hundred and sixty men were at the workings. Everybody got out though young Isambard had to go back to rescue others.

He wasted no time in attacking the disaster. From the West India Dock Company he borrowed a diving bell to inspect the hole in the river-bed, and afterwards recorded it all in his journal: "What a dream it now appears to me! Going down in the diving-bell, finding and examining the hole! The novelty of the thing, the excitement of the occasional risk. . . the crowds of boats to witness our works. . . ."

He also took a boat down inside the workings to inspect the flood within the Tunnel. He made sketches of this hazardous trip and afterwards wrote of it ecstatically:

. . .the hollow rushing of water; the total darkness of all around rendered distinct by the glimmering light of a candle or two, carried by ourselves. . . a dark recess at the end – quite dark – water rushing from it in such quantities as to render it uncertain whether the ground was secure. . . a cavern, *huge, misshapen* with water – a cataract coming from it – candles going out. . . .

Incredibly, distinguished sightseers continued to arrive and, presumably as a kind of public relations exercise, young Brunel took them into the flooded workings – even Charles Bonaparte, a non-swimmer, accompanied by the geologist Sir Roderick Murchison who left his own hilarious account of the visit.

The first operation we underwent (one which I never repeated) was to go down in a diving-bell upon the cavity by which the Thames had broken in. Buckland and Featherstonehaugh, having been the first to volunteer, came up with such red faces and such staring eyes, that I felt no great inclination to follow their example, particularly as Charles Bonaparte was most anxious to avoid the dilemma, excusing himself by saying that his family were very short-necked and subject to apoplexy, etc.; but it would not do to show the white feather; I got in, and induced him to follow me. The effect was, as I expected, most oppressive, and then on the bottom what did we see but dirty gravel and mud, from which I brought up a fragment of one of Hunt's blacking bottles. We soon pulled the string, and were delighted to breathe the fresh air.

The first folly was, however, quite overpowered by the next. We went down the shaft on the south bank, and got, with young Brunel, into a punt, which he was to steer into the tunnel till we reached the repairing shield. About eleven feet of water were still in the tunnel, leaving just space enough above our heads for Brunel to stand up and claw the ceiling and sides to impel us. As we were proceeding he called out, "Now, gentlemen, if by accident there should be a rush of water, I shall turn the punt over and prevent you being jammed against the roof, and we shall then be carried out and up the shaft!" On this C. Bonaparte remarked, "But I cannot swim!" and, just as he had said the words, Brunel, swinging carelessly from right to left, fell overboard, and out went the candles with which he was lighting up the place. Taking this for the *sauve qui peut*, fat C.B., then the very image of Napoleon at St Helena, was about to roll after him, when I held him fast, and, by the glimmering light from the entrance, we found young Brunel, who swam like a fish, coming up on the other side of the punt, and soon got him on board. We of course called out for an immediate retreat, for really there could not be a more foolhardy and ridiculous risk of our lives, inasmuch as it was just the moment of trial as to whether the Thames would make a further inroad or not.

Foolhardiness was to continue. Directors of the Tunnel Company, conducted by young Brunel and an escort of miners, were taking a boat trip to inspect the flooded workings when one of them, a Mr Martin, suddenly stood up in the boat and struck his head on the tunnel roof. He fell backwards against his companions capsizing the boat. Like most of the party Martin was a non-swimmer, and there followed a desperate struggle in the water. In spite of the life-saving efforts of young Isambard one of the miners was drowned.

While the Tunnel was being cleared in August 1827 the elder Brunel, harassed by financial worries as the flooding diminished their capital, took to his bed, handing over the superintendence of the work to young Isambard who – at the age of twenty-one – became Resident Engineer.

After a few months of renewed work there was another dramatic exercise in public relations. The sides of the arches were hung with crimson draperies and long tables

were laid for dinner – for fifty distinguished guests in one arch and for a hundred and twenty of the workpeople in the adjoining arch. A special feature of the occasion was that the scene was brilliantly lit by great candelabra of a new "portable gas". The band of the Coldstream Guards provided musical entertainment. The reason for this extravaganza was to reassure the financial backers and the public in general that the Tunnel was fully restored and that progress was being made.

Toward the middle of January 1828, however, the river broke in again and this time young Brunel himself was a casualty. During his convalescence, he wrote this account of the catastrophe.

I have now been laid up quite useless for 14 weeks and upwards, ever since the 14th January. I shan't forget that day in a hurry, very near finished my journey then; when the danger is over, it is rather amusing than otherwise – while it existed I can't say the feeling was at all uncomfortable. If I was to say the contrary, I should be nearer the truth in this instance. While exertions could still be made and hope remained of stopping the ground it was an excitement which has always been a luxury to me. When we were obliged to run, I felt nothing in particular; I was only thinking of the best way of getting us on and the probable state of the arches. When knocked down, I certainly gave myself up, but I took it very much as a matter of course, which I had expected the moment we quitted the frames, for I never expected we should get out. The instant I disengaged myself and got breath again – all dark – I bolted into the other arch – this saved me by laying hold of the railrope – the engine *must* have stopped a minute. I stood still nearly a minute. I was anxious for poor Ball and Collins, who I felt too sure had never risen from the fall we had all had and were, as I thought, *crushed* under the great stage. I kept calling them by name to encourage them and make them also (if still able) come through the opening. While standing there the effect was – *grand* – the roar of the rushing water in a confined passage, and by its velocity rushing past the opening was grand, *very grand*. I cannot compare it to anything, cannon can be nothing to it. At last it came bursting through the opening. I was then obliged to be off – but up to that moment, as far as my sensations were concerned, and distinct from the idea of the loss of six poor fellows whose death I could not then foresee, kept there.

This inundation resulted in seven years of suspended operations during which the tunnel still remained a spectacle, the workings being sealed off and covered by a great mirror before which the public paid to gaze and wonder.

Young Isambard allowed a touch of facetiousness to temper his despair.

The young Rennies, whatever their real merit, will have built London Bridge, the finest bridge in Europe, and have such a connection with government as to defy competition. Palmer has built new London Docks and thus without labour has established a connection which ensures his fortune, while I – shall have been engaged on the Tunnel which failed, which was abandoned – a pretty recommendation. . . .

I'll turn misanthrope, get a huge Meerschaum, as big as myself and smoke away melancholy – and yet that can't be done without money and that can't be got without working for it. Dear me, what a world this is where starvation itself is an expensive luxury. But damn all croaking, the Tunnel must go on, it shall go on. . . .

He could not of course be expected to live with the Tunnel failure even if it was temporary. He realised that it was necessary in those pioneering, competitive times to build some reputation for himself at once, so he worked at first on a brain child of his father's – a projected "gaz engine" – obtaining power by generating gas from carbonate of ammonia and sulphuric acid, which was passed over condensers. The experimental plant had been laid down at Rotherhithe on the site of the Tunnel workings, and in April 1829 young Isambard was writing: "Here I am at Rotherhithe, renewing experiments on gaz – been getting the apparatus up for the last *six months*!! Is it possible? A $1/40$ of the remainder of my life – what a life, the life of a dreamer – am always building castles in the air, what time I waste!" Indeed, it was wasted time. The "gaz" experiments were abandoned in 1833, when he wrote: "All the time and expense, both *enormous*, devoted to this thing for nearly 10 years are therefore *wasted.* . . . It must therefore die and with it all my fine hopes – crash – gone – well, well, it can't be helped."

He was by no means confined to Rotherhithe or to his father's affairs. Without the benefit of railways, he demonstrated unusual mobility, a characteristic of his later life. He was concerned with drainage works at Tollesbury on the Essex coast in 1830 and the following year with the construction of a new dock at Monkwearmouth, Sunderland. Towards the end of that year he covered 528 miles by road sightseeing bridges, cathedrals, docks and at Liverpool took his first journey on the railroad. Two jobs which cropped up in London were disappointing. At Woolwich he made surveys and trial borings for a new dry dock for the Navy Board, who turned him down. At Kensington he worked on the design and construction of an observatory for Sir James South. This was successful enough in itself, being completed in May 1831 with a dinner in celebration at which Brunel in his own words was "lionized". But Sir James South declared that the work had exceeded the original estimate and tried to refuse to pay for it. The *Athenaeum*, in an article possibly written by Sir James himself, declared the construction of the observatory to be "an absurd project" having "no other object than the display of a *tour de force*, and... an effort to produce effect on the part of the architect". Young Brunel himself was quite capable of dishing out adverse criticism. Asked for his opinion of John Nash's work on the future Buckingham Palace, he declared it to be "an extraordinary, iniquitous, jobbing, tasteless, unskilful, profligate waste of money. Walls without foundation, ornament without meaning – job, job, job. . . ."

An important ingredient of his character emerges from this period so cluttered with frustration and disappointment – ability to write off loss. He must often have repeated to himself what he wrote about the "gaz engine": "all my fine hopes – crash – gone." Just as often he must have added to himself, "well, well, it can't be helped." The acceptance of failure, with a resolve to change course, or to try again, or to do something else, was part of the momentum of his life – and it also contributed to the remarkable vitality and flexibility of his times.

The Tunnel went on with Treasury aid seven years later. In March 1843, by which time young Isambard had fathered Isambard III and was a national figure in his own right, *The Times* reported: "The ceremony of throwing open this 'great bore' to the public was performed on Saturday last under favour of good-natured old Father Thames." Fifty thousand people paid their pennies to go through within twenty-seven hours of the official opening.

Though Queen Victoria herself walked through it and knighted Marc Isambard, it was only a partial triumph. The horse traffic which was to relieve London's transport never went through. It remained a pedestrian crossing with a sideline of public entertainment, a lurking place not always wholly respectable, until it was taken over by railway interests in the late 1860s; it remains to this day part of London's Underground Railway system.

ADVENTURE IN THE CRIMEA

MARY SEACOLE

from Wonderful Adventures of Mrs Seacole

Although never a slave herself, Mary Seacole was born into Jamaican slave society. She was an incredible entrepreneur, embarking on careers as a traveller, businesswoman, gold prospector, nurse and eventually writer. In 1857 she published her autobiography. One of the most exciting and moving episodes concerns her adventures in the Crimean War where she set up a canteen medical centre and accommodation for offices called the British Hotel. In the first extract, Mrs Seacole vividly writes about her first impressions of the Crimea.

THE VERY FIRST DAY that I approached the wharf, a party of sick and wounded had just arrived. Here was work for me, I felt sure. With so many patients, the doctors must be glad of all the hands they could get. Indeed, so strong was the old impulse within me, that I waited for no permission, but seeing a poor artilleryman stretched upon a pallet, groaning heavily, I ran up to him at once, and eased the stiff dressings. Lightly my practised fingers ran over the familiar work,

and well was I rewarded when the poor fellow's groans subsided into a restless uneasy mutter. God help him! He had been hit in the forehead, and I think his sight was gone. I stooped down, and raised some tea to his baked lips (here and there upon the wharf were rows of little pannikins containing this beverage). Then his hand touched mine, and rested there, and I heard him mutter indistinctly, as though the discovery had arrested his wandering senses – "Ha! this is surely a woman's hand."

I couldn't say much, but I tried to whisper something about hope and trust in God; but all the while I think his thoughts were running on this strange discovery. Perhaps I had brought to his poor mind memories of his home, and the loving ones there, who would ask no greater favour than the privilege of helping him thus; for he continued to hold my hand in his feeble grasp, and whisper "God bless you, *woman* – whoever you are, God bless you!" – over and over again.

I do not think that the surgeons noticed me at first, although, as this was my introduction to Balaclava, I had not neglected my personal appearance, and wore my favourite yellow dress, and blue bonnet, with the red ribbons; but I noticed one coming to me, who, I think, would have laughed very merrily had it not been for the poor fellow at my feet. As it was, he came forward, and shook hands very kindly, saying, "How do you do, ma'am? Much obliged to you for looking after my poor fellow; very glad to see you here." And glad they always were, the kind-hearted doctors, to let me help them look after the sick and wounded sufferers brought to that fearful wharf.

I wonder if I can ever forget the scenes I witnessed there? Oh! they were heartrending. I declare that I saw rough bearded men stand by and cry like the softest-hearted women at the sights of suffering they saw; while some who scorned comfort for themselves, would fidget about for hours before the long trains of mules and ambulances came in, nervous lest the most trifling thing that could minister to the sufferers' comfort should be neglected. I have often heard men talk and preach very learnedly and conclusively about the great wickedness and selfishness of the human heart; I used to wonder whether they would have modified those opinions if they had been my companions for one day of the six weeks I spent upon that wharf, and seen but one day's experience of the Christian sympathy and brotherly love shown by the strong to the weak. The task was a trying one, and familiarity, you might think, would have worn down their keener feelings of pity and sympathy; but it was not so.

I was in the midst of my sad work one day when the Admiral came up, and stood looking on. He vouchsafed no word nor look of recognition in answer to my salute, but stood silently by, his hands behind his back, watching the sick being lifted into the boats. You might have thought that he had little feeling, so stern and expressionless was his face; but once, when they raised a sufferer somewhat awkwardly, and he groaned deeply, that rough man broke out all at once with an oath, that was strangely like a prayer, and bade the men, for God's sake, take more care. And, coming up to me, he clapped me on the shoulder, saying, "I am glad to see you here, old lady, among these poor fellows;" while, I am most strangely deceived if I did not see a tear-drop gathering in his eye. It was on this same day, I think, that bending down over a poor fellow whose senses had quite gone, and, I fear me, would never return to him in this world, he took me for his wife, and calling me "Mary, Mary," many times, asked me how it was he had got home so quickly, and why he did not see the children; and said he felt sure he should soon get better now. Poor fellow! I could not undeceive him. I think the fancy happily caused by the touch of a woman's hand soothed his dying hour; for I do not fancy he could have lived to reach Scutari. I never knew it for certain, but I always felt sure that he would never wake from that dream of home in this world.

And here, lest the reader should consider that I am speaking too highly of my own actions, I must have recourse to a plan which I shall frequently adopt in the following pages, and let another voice speak for me in the kind letter received long after Balaclava had been left to its old. masters, by one who had not forgotten his old companion on the sick-wharf. The writer Major (then Captain) R—, had charge of the wharf while I was there.

"Glasgow, Sept. 1856.

Dear Mrs Seacole, – I am very sorry to hear that you have been unfortunate in business; but I am glad to hear that you have found friends in Lord R— and others, who are ready to help you. No one knows better than I do how much you did to help poor sick and wounded soldiers; and I feel sure you will find in your day of trouble that they have not forgotten it."

Major R— was a brave and experienced officer, but the scenes on the sick-wharf unmanned him often. I have know him nervously restless if the people were behind-hand, even for a few minutes, in their preparations for the wounded. But in this feeling all shared alike. Only women could have done more than they did who attended to this melancholy duty; and they, not because their hearts could be softer, but because their hands are moulded for this work.

But it must not be supposed that we had no cheerful scenes upon the sick-wharf. Sometimes a light-hearted fellow – generally a sailor – would forget his pain, and do his best to keep the rest in good spirits. Once I heard my name eagerly pronounced, and turning round, recognized a sailor whom I remembered as one of the crew of the "Alarm," stationed at Kingston, a few years back.

"Why, as I live, if this ain't Aunty Seacole, of Jamaica! Shiver all that's left of my poor timbers" – and I saw that the left leg was gone – "if this ain't a rum go, mates!"

"Ah! my man, I'm sorry to see you in this sad plight."

"Never fear for me, Aunty Seacole; I'll make the best of the leg the Rooshians have left me. I'll get at them soon again, never fear. You don't think, mess-mates" – he never left his wounded comrades alone – "that they'll think less of us at home for coming back with a limb or so short?"

"You bear your troubles well, my son."

"Eh! do I, Aunty?" and he seemed surprised. "Why, look'ye, when I've seen so many pretty fellows knocked off the ship's roll altogether, don't you think I ought to be thankful if I can answer the bo'swain's call anyhow?"

And this was the sailors' philosophy always. And this brave fellow, after he had sipped some lemonade, and laid down, when he heard the men groaning, raised his head and comforted them in the same strain again; and, it may seem strange, but it quieted them.

I used to make sponge-cakes on board the "Medora," with eggs brought from Constantinople. Only the other day, Captain S—, who had charge of the "Medora," reminded me of them. These, with some lemonade, were all the doctors would allow me to give to the wounded. They all liked the cake, poor fellows, better than anything else: perhaps because it tasted of "home."

Once her centre was established, Mary Seacole described a typical day of her life in the Crimea.

I should like, with the reader's permission, to describe one day of my life in the Crimea. They were all pretty much alike, except when there was fighting upon a large scale going on, and duty called me to the field. I was generally up and busy by daybreak, sometimes earlier, for in the summer my bed had no attractions strong enough to bind me to it after four. There was plenty to do before the work of the day began. There was the poultry to pluck and prepare for cooking, which had been killed on the previous night; the joints to be cut up and got ready for the same purpose; the medicines to be mixed; the store to be swept and cleaned. Of very great importance, with all these things to see after, were the few hours of quiet before the road became alive with travellers. By seven o'clock the morning coffee would be ready, hot and refreshing, and eagerly sought for by the officers of the Army Works

Corps engaged upon making the great highroad to the front, and the Commissariat and Land Transport men carrying stores from Balaclava to the heights. There was always a great demand for coffee by those who knew its refreshing and strengthening qualities, milk I could not give them (I kept it [in] tins for special use); but they had it hot and strong, with plenty of sugar and a slice of butter, which I recommend as a capital substitute for milk. From that time until nine, officers on duty in the neighbourhood, or passing by, would look in for breakfast, and about half-past nine my sick patients began to show themselves. In the following hour they came thickly, and sometimes it was past twelve before I had got through this duty. They came with every variety of suffering and disease; the cases I most disliked were the frostbitten fingers and feet in the winter. That over, there was the hospital to visit across the way, which was sometimes overcrowded with patients. I was a good deal there, and as often as possible would take over books and papers, which I used to borrow for that purpose from my friends and the officers I knew. Once, a great packet of tracts was sent to me from Plymouth anonymously, and these I distributed in the same manner. By this time the day's news had come from the front, and perhaps among the casualties over night there would be some one wounded or sick, who would be glad to see me ride up with the comforts he stood most in need of; and during the day, if any accident occurred in the neighbourhood or on the road near the British Hotel, the men generally brought the sufferer there, whence, if the hurt was serious, he would be transferred to the hospital of the Land Transport opposite. I used not always to stand upon too much ceremony when I heard of sick or wounded officers in the front. Sometimes their friends would ask me to go to them, though very often I waited for no hint, but took the chance of meeting with a kind reception. I used to think of their relatives at home, who would have given so much to possess my privilege; and more than one officer have I startled by appearing before him, and telling him abruptly that he must have a mother, wife, or sister at home whom he missed, and that he must therefore be glad of some woman to take their place.

Until evening the store would be filled with customers wanting stores, dinners, and luncheons; loungers and idlers seeking conversation and amusement; and at eight o'clock the curtain descended on that day's labour, and I could sit down and eat at leisure. It was no easy thing to clear the store, canteen, and yards; but we determined upon adhering to the rule that nothing should be sold after that hour, and succeeded. Any one who came after that time, came simply as a friend. There could be no necessity for any one, except on extraordinary occasions, when the rule could be relaxed, to purchase things after eight o'clock. And drunkenness or excess were discouraged at Spring Hill in every way; indeed, my few unpleasant scenes arose chiefly from my refusing to sell liquor where I saw it was wanted to be abused. I could appeal with a clear conscience to all who knew me there, to back my assertion that I neither permitted drunkenness among the men nor gambling among the officers. Whatever happened elsewhere, intoxication, cards, and dice were never to be seen within the precincts of the British Hotel. My regulations were well known, and a kind-hearted officer of the Royals who was much there, and who permitted me to use a familiarity towards him which I trust I never abused, undertook to be my Provost-marshall, but his duties were very light.

At first we kept our store open on Sunday from sheer necessity, but after a little while, when stores in abundance were established at Kadikoi and elsewhere, and the absolute necessity no longer existed, Sunday became a day of most grateful rest at Spring Hill. This step also met with opposition from the men; but again we were determined, and again we triumphed. I am sure we needed rest. I have often wondered since how it was that I never fell ill or came home "on urgent private affairs." I am afraid that I was not sufficiently thankful to the Providence which gave me strength to carry out the work I loved so well, and felt so happy in being engaged upon; but although I never had a week's illness during my campaign, the labour, anxiety, and perhaps the few trials that followed it, have told upon me. I have never felt since that time the strong and hearty woman that I was when I braved with impunity the pestilence of Navy Bay and Cruces. It would kill me easily now.

As the war progressed, Mrs Seacole became deeply moved by the deaths in the trenches.

It was very usual, when a young officer was ordered into the trenches, for him to ride down to Spring Hill to dine, or obtain something more than his ordinary fare to brighten his weary hours in those fearful ditches. They seldom failed on these occasions to shake me by the hand

at parting, and sometimes would say, "You see, Mrs
Seacole, I can't say goodbye to the dear ones at home, so
I'll bid you goodbye for them. Perhaps you'll see them
some day, and if the Russians should knock me over,
mother, just tell them I thought of them all – will you?"
And although all this might be said in a light-hearted
manner, it was rather solemn. I felt it to be so, for I never
failed (although who was I, that I should preach?) to say
something about God's providence and relying upon it;
and they were very good. No army of parsons could be
much better than my sons. They would listen very gravely,
and shake me by the hand again, while I felt that there was
nothing in the world I would not do for them. Then very
often the men would say, "I'm going in with my master
tonight, Mrs Seacole; come and look after him, if he's hit;"
and so often as this happened I would pass the night
restlessly, awaiting with anxiety the morning, and yet
dreading to hear the news it held in store for me. I used to
think it was like having a large family of children ill with
fever, and dreading to hear which one had passed away in
the night.

And as often as the bad news came, I thought it my duty

to ride up to the hut of the sufferer and do my woman's work. But I felt it deeply. How could it be otherwise? There was one poor boy in the Artillery, with blue eyes and light golden hair, whom I nursed through a long and weary sickness, borne with all a man's spirit, and whom I grew to love like a fond old-fashioned mother. I thought if ever angels watched over any life, they would shelter his; but one day, but a short time after he had left his sick-bed, he was struck down on his battery, working like a young hero. It was a long time before I could banish from my mind the thought of him as I saw him last, the yellow hair, stiff and stained with his life-blood, and the blue eyes closed in the sleep of death. Of course, I saw him buried, as I did poor H— V—, my old Jamaica friend, whose kind face was so familiar to me of old. Another good friend I mourned bitterly – Captain B—, of the Coldstreams – a great cricketer. He had been with me on the previous evening, had seemed dull, but had supped at my store, and on the following morning a brother officer told me he was shot dead while setting his pickets*, which made me ill and unfit for work for the whole day. Mind you, a day was a long time to give to sorrow in the Crimea.

I could give many other similar instances, but why should I sadden myself or my readers? Others have described the horrors of those fatal trenches; but their real history has never been written, and perhaps it is as well that so harrowing a tale should be left in oblivion. Such anecdotes as the following were very current in the Camp, but I have no means of answering for its truth. Two sergeants met in the trenches, who had been school-mates in their youth; years had passed since they set out for the battle of life by different roads, and now they met again under the fire of a common enemy. With one impulse they started forward to exchange the hearty hand-shake and the mutual greetings, and while their hands were still clasped, a chance shot killed both.

* *Setting pickets: posting groups of sentries for the night.*

Brave as ever, Mrs Seacole entered Sebastopol as it was being evacuated.

For weeks past I had been offering bets to every one that I would not only be the first woman to enter Sebastopol from the English lines, but that I would be the first to carry refreshments into the fallen city. And now the time I had longed for had come. I borrowed some mules from the Land Transport Corps – mine were knocked up by yesterday's work – and loading them with good things, started off with my partner and some other friends early on that memorable Sunday morning for Cathcart's Hill.

When I found that strict orders had been given to admit no one inside Sebastopol, I became quite excited; and making my way to General Garrett's quarters, I made such an earnest representation of what I considered my right that I soon obtained a pass, of which the following is a copy:-

"Pass Mrs Seacole and her attendants, with refreshments for officers and soldiers in the Redan and in Sebastopol.

Garrett, M.G.

Cathcart's Hill, Sept. 9, 1855."

So many attached themselves to my staff, becoming for the nonce my attendants, that I had some difficulty at starting; but at last I passed all the sentries safely, much to the annoyance of many officers, who were trying every conceivable scheme to evade them, and entered the city. I can give you no very clear description of its condition on that Sunday morning, a year and a half ago. Many parts of it were still blazing furiously – explosions were taking place in all directions – every step had a score of dangers; and yet curiosity and excitement carried us on and on. I was often stopped to give refreshments to officers and men, who had been fasting for hours. Some, on the other hand, had found their way to Russian cellars; and one body of men were most ingloriously drunk, and playing the wildest pranks. They were dancing, yelling, and singing – some of them with Russian women's dresses

fastened round their waists, and old bonnets stuck upon
their heads.

I was offered many trophies. All plunder was stopped
by the sentries, and confiscated, so that the soldiers could
afford to be liberal. By one I was offered a great velvet
sofa; another pressed a huge armchair, which had graced
some Sebastopol study, upon me: while a third begged my
acceptance of a portion of a grand piano. What I did carry
away was very unimportant; a gaily-decorated altar-
candle, studded with gold and silver stars, which the
present Commander-in-Chief condescended to accept as a
Sebastopol memorial; an old cracked China teapot, which
in happier times had very likely dispensed pleasure to
many a small tea-party; a cracked bell, which had rung
many to prayers during the siege, and which I bore away
on my saddle; and a parasol, given me by a drunken
soldier. He had a silk skirt on, and torn lace upon his
wrists, and he came mincingly up, holding the parasol
above his head, and imitating the walk of an affected lady,
to the vociferous delight of his comrades. And all this, and
much more, in that fearful charnel city, with death and
suffering on every side.

It was very hazardous to pass along some of the streets
exposed to the fire of the Russians on the north side of the

harbour. We had to wait and watch our opportunity, and then gallop for it. Some of us had close shaves of being hit. More than this, fires still kept breaking out around; while mines and fougasses not unfrequently exploded from unknown causes. We saw two officers emerge from a heap of ruins, covered and almost blinded with smoke and dust, from some such unlooked-for explosion. With considerable difficulty we succeeded in getting into the quarter of the town held by the French, where I was nearly getting into serious trouble.

I had loitered somewhat behind my party, watching, with pardonable curiosity, the adroitness with which a party of French were plundering a house; and by the time my curiosity had been satisfied, I found myself quite alone, my retinue having preceded me by some few hundred yards. This would have been of little consequence, had not an American sailor lad, actuated either by mischief or folly, whispered to the Frenchmen that I was a Russian spy; and had they not, instead laughing at him, credited his assertion, and proceeded to arrest me. Now, such a charge was enough to make a lion of a lamb; so I refused positively to dismount, and made matters worse by knocking in the cap of the first soldier who laid hands upon me, with the bell that hung at my saddle. Upon this, six or seven tried to force me to the guard-house in rather a rough manner, while I resisted with all my force, screaming out for Mr Day, and using the bell for a weapon. How I longed for a better one I need not tell the reader. In the midst of this scene came up a French officer, whom I recognised as the patient I had taken to Spring Hill after the battle of the Tchernaya, and who took my part at once, and ordered them to release me. Although I rather weakened my cause, it was most natural that, directly I was released, I should fly at the varlet who had caused me this trouble; and I did so, using my bell most effectually, and aided, when my party returned, by their riding-whips.

This little adventure took up altogether so much time that, when the French soldiers had made their apologies to me, and I had returned the compliment to the one whose head had been dented by my bell, it was growing late, and we made our way back to Cathcart's Hill. On the way, a little French soldier begged hard of me to buy a picture, which had been cut from above the altar of some church in Sebastopol. It was too dark to see much of his prize, but I ultimately became its possessor, and brought it home with me. It is some eight or ten feet in length, and represents, I should think, the Madonna. I am no judge of such things, but I think, although the painting is rather coarse, that the face of the Virgin, and the heads of Cherubim that fill the cloud from which she is descending, are soft and beautiful. There is a look of divine calmness and heavenly love in the Madonna's face which is very striking; and, perhaps, during the long and awful siege many a knee was bent in worship before it, and many a heart found comfort in its soft loving gaze.

FIRST ON THE MOON

GENE FARMER and DORA JANE HAMBLING

*Neil Armstrong, Edwin E. (Buzz) Aldrin and Michael Collins
were the astronauts of the Apollo 11 Space Mission to the Moon.
Armstrong and Aldrin, the first men on the Moon, landed the
Lunar Module, Eagle, in the Mare Tranquilitatis on 20 June 1969,
while Collins remained in orbit in the Command Module,
Columbia. Armstrong and Aldrin spent 2hrs 13mins and 1hr
43mins respectively on the surface and collected 21kg of soil and
small rocks for laboratory analysis. The three astronauts returned
safely to Earth on 24 July.*

I N A SLEEPY VALLEY called Honeysuckle Creek, named for the plant which abounds in that rugged area twenty-five miles from the Australian national capital, Canberra, some one hundred technicians were gathered around two giant screens. They were waiting to receive – and relay to the rest of the world – the first television pictures of man on the moon. Because of the relative positions of the earth and the moon at the time Armstrong and Aldrin were to step out of the lunar module and onto the moon, the television relay was Honeysuckle's job. Honeysuckle, built by NASA in 1966 at a cost of some two million dollars [Australian], was actually part of a chain of three Australian tracking stations. Backing up Honeysuckle's 85-foot diameter antenna "dish", rising 114 feet in the air, were facilities at nearby Tidbinbilla and at Parkes, more than one hundred miles away in New South

Wales, where an even bigger antenna – 210 feet, largest in the southern hemisphere – had been borrowed from the Commonwealth Scientific and Industrial Research Organization (CSIRO) to receive signals from Apollo 11 during its journey to the moon. Both the Honeysuckle and Parkes antennae were ready to start receiving – and relaying – pictures when the moon walk began. There was a discernible tension among the technicians, most of them – like their Houston counterparts – surprisingly young, many of them wearing beards. They had tracked other missions, but, said station administrative officer Bernie Scrivener, "Somehow this seemed to be so much more important. Since the Apollo 7 mission, this was the day for which everyone on the station had worked and trained." Supervising technician Laurie Turner, who had to process data related to the heartbeats of the astronauts during the moon walk and on the condition of their backpacks, confessed to a feeling of genuine anxiety: "Not for the safety of the astronauts. I think we all had faith in the technology which put them there, but I was anxious for myself. Would the tests and simulations we had performed *really* be like the thing itself? Or would critical adjustments or repatching of circuits be necessary to get the vital data back to Houston?" And the week had not been without its crises. On the third day of the mission Tidbinbilla messaged: "We have lost both our transmitters – suspected power failure." It turned out that only one transmitter had been lost, but a prodigious effort had to be made to repair the other – the nearest available spare parts were at the Woomera rocket range, nearly a thousand miles away in the desert. Hard work and the cooperation of a domestic airline got the job done less than twenty-four hours before the lunar landing. As the staffs of all three stations waited for the moon walk, Dr E. G. ("Taffy") Bowen, a world figure in radio astronomy who directed CSRIO's radiophysics division at Parkes, remarked, "Our only worry now is the weather or some event we can't foresee." Shortly afterward there was bad news: a serious squall was approaching from the north-west. A few minutes later it hit Parkes's giant dish with a 35-mph gust, threatening to put the whole station out of commission. Dr Bowen made no effort to conceal his worry as the dish shook under the wind's impact. But it held, and the tracking continued as the world waited.

HOUSTON (McCandless): Neil, this is Houston. What's your status on hatch open? Over.

EAGLE (Armstrong): Everything is go here. We're just waiting for the cabin pressure to bleed so – to blow enough pressure to open the hatch. It's about .1 on our gauge now.

EAGLE (Aldrin): Sure hate to tug on that thing [the hatch handle]. Alternative would be to open the overhead hatch too.

Past nine-thirty in the evening, Houston time. . .

HOUSTON (McCandless): We're showing a relatively static pressure on your cabin. Do you think you can open the hatch at this pressure?

EAGLE (Armstrong): We're going to try it.

EAGLE (Aldrin): The hatch is opening.

EAGLE (Armstrong): The hatch is open!

ARMSTRONG: "Is my antenna out? Okay, now we're ready to hook up the LEC here." ALDRIN: "Now that should go down. . . [*static*]. . . Put the bag up this way. That's even. Neil, are you hooked up to it?" ARMSTRONG: "Yes. Okay. Now we need to hook this." ALDRIN: "Leave that up there." ARMSTRONG: "Yes." ALDRIN: "Okay, your visor down? Your back is up against the. . . [*static*]. . . All right, now it's on top of the DSKY. Forward and up, now you're there, over toward me, straight down, relax a little bit. . . Neil, you're lined up nicely. Toward me a little bit. Okay, down. Okay, made it clear. . . [*static*]. . ."

ALDRIN: "Move. Here, roll to the left. Okay, now you're clear. You're lined up on the platform. Put your left foot to the right a little bit. Okay, that's good. Roll left." ARMSTRONG: "Okay, now I'm going to check the ingress here." ALDRIN: "Okay, not quite squared away. Roll to the – roll right a little. Now you're even." ARMSTRONG: "That's okay?" ALDRIN: "That's good. You've got plenty of room." ARMSTRONG: "How am I doing?" ALDRIN: "You're doing fine... Okay, do you want those bags?" ARMSTRONG: "Yes. Got it.... Okay, Houston, I'm on the porch.".... [*Nine ladder steps to the moon...*]

HOUSTON (McCandless): Roger, Neil.... Columbia, Columbia, this is Houston. One minute and thirty seconds to LOS. All systems go. Over.... [*Goodbye to Mike Collins for another forty-five minutes.... Neil Armstrong on the porch at 109 hours 19 minutes and 16 seconds GET...*]

And from TRANQUILITY:

ARMSTRONG: "You need more slack, Buzz?" ALDRIN: "No, hold it just a minute." ARMSTRONG: "Okay." [*Twenty-five minutes of PLSS time expended...*] ALDRIN: "Okay, everything's nice and straight in here." ARMSTRONG: "Okay, can you pull the door open a little more?" ALDRIN: "Did you get the MESA out?" ARMSTRONG: "I'm going to pull it now." ARMSTRONG: "Houston, the MESA came down all right."

HOUSTON: (McCandless): Roger, we copy, and we're standing by for your TV. [*So were millions of other people. . . people looking at giant screens in Trafalgar Square, London, and in Seoul, Korea. . .*]

HOUSTON (McCandless): Neil, this is Houston. You're loud and clear. Break, break. Buzz, this is Houston. Radio check and verify TV circuit breaker in.

EAGLE (Aldrin): Roger. TV circuit breaker's in. LMP reads loud and clear.

HOUSTON (McCandless): And we're getting a picture on the TV.

EAGLE (Aldrin): Oh, you got a good picture. Huh?

In the briefing room at Honeysuckle Creek, Australia, where the picture was seen first – it was Neil Armstrong's leg – a voice in the back broke the silence: "Who said we'd miss it?" There was an anonymous answer from somewhere else in the room: "We've got it, all right." Ed Renouard, the scan converter technician at Honeysuckle Creek, breathed a little easier: "When I was sitting there in front of the converter, waiting for a pattern on the input monitor, I was hardly aware of the rest of the world. I remembered how smoothly Apollo 10 had gone. But that was Apollo 10 – straightforward commercial TV which needed only proven techniques. Today we really fired 'The Beast' in earnest, and suddenly all those long hours of training seemed worth it. I heard Buzz Aldrin say 'TV circuit breaker in,' and suddenly on the screen I saw the sloping strut of the lunar module's leg against the moon's surface." Bernie Scrivener remembered, "I just paused and wondered. It was hard to tear yourself away from that screen and get back to your job."

HOUSTON (McCandless): Okay, Neil, we can see you coming down the ladder now.

EAGLE (Armstrong): Okay, I just checked – getting back up to that first step, Buzz, it's not even collapsed too far, but it's adequate to get back up.... It takes a pretty good little jump.... I'm at the foot of the ladder. The LM footpads are only depressed in the surface about one or two inches. Although the surface appears to be very, very fine-grained, as you get close to it. It's almost like a powder. Now and then, it's very fine... I'm going to step off the LM now... [*I had thought about what I was going to say, largely because so many people had asked me to think about it. I thought about that a little bit on the way to the moon, and it wasn't really decided until after we got onto the lunar surface. I guess I hadn't actually decided what I wanted to say until just before we went out...*]

In El Lago Jan Armstrong bent down to explain to her

son Mark why his father had to move around slowly: "The suit is very heavy and the sun is very hot, like Texas. He has to be careful because if he tears his suit it could be very, very bad." Mark rubbed his eyes. At 9.55.10 p.m. Houston time, Mark pointed to the television screen. His father was coming down the ladder of the lunar module. "I don't see it," Mark complained. When Neil described the fine-grained soil, Mark asked, "How come I can't see him?" Jan Armstrong smiled and encouraged her husband from a quarter of a million miles away: "Be descriptive." In Nassau Bay Joan Aldrin clapped her hands and said, "Look, look! Gee... I can't believe this." In the Collins home there was a babble of conversation: "I see something moving. I can't stand it." "This is science fiction." "It looks like the North Pole." "Let's listen for his first words...."

At 9.56 p.m., Houston time, Neil Armstrong stepped out of the dish-shaped landing pad and onto the surface of the moon. "THAT'S ONE SMALL STEP FOR A MAN, ONE GIANT LEAP FOR MANKIND."

The quality of the television transmission delighted everyone in the world.

It was time for Neil Armstrong to walk on the moon, and as Armstrong waited for Aldrin to follow him out in nineteen minutes his first reaction to the environment was a favourable one. He was able immediately to discard the theory, once widely held, that the windless surface of the moon was overlaid with a dangerously deep coating of dust in which men and man-made machines would founder. The lunar module's footpads had made only a shallow penetration, and Neil's boots sank only a fraction of an inch: "Maybe an eighth of an inch, but I can see the footprints of my boots and the treads in the fine sandy particles." And he could move around: "There seems to be no difficulty.... It's even perhaps easier than the simulations at one-sixth G.... It's actually no trouble to walk around. The descent engine did not leave a crater of any size. There's about one foot clearance on the ground. We're essentially on a very level place here. I can see some evidence of rays emanating from the descent engine, but very insignificant amounts.... Okay, Buzz, we're ready to bring down the camera."

"I'm all ready," Aldrin answered.... "Okay, you'll have to pay out all the LEC [lunar equipment conveyor]. It looks like it's coming out nice and evenly."

"Okay, it's quite dark here in the shadow and a little hard for me to see if I have good footing. I'll work my way over into the sunlight here without looking directly into the sun."

"Okay, it's taut now," Aldrin said. "Don't hold it quite so tight."

Armstrong looked up at the LM and messaged: "I'm standing directly in the shadow now, looking up at Buzz in the window. And I can see everything clearly. The light is sufficiently bright, backlighted into the front of the LM, that everything is very clearly visible."

"Okay, I'm going to be changing this film magazine," Aldrin said.

"Okay," Armstrong said. "Camera installed on the RCU bracket [remote control unit]. I'm storing the LEC on the secondary strut. . . I'll step out and take some of my first pictures here."

HOUSTON (McCandless): Roger, Neil, we're reading you loud and clear. We see you getting some pictures and the contingency sample.

"This is very interesting," Armstrong said. "It's a very soft surface, but here and there where I plug with the contingency sample collector, I run into a very hard surface. . . . I'll try to get a rock in here. Here's a couple."

"That looks beautiful from here, Neil," Aldrin said from Eagle's cabin.

"It has a stark beauty all its own. It's like much of the high desert of the United States. It's different, but its very pretty out here."

In El Lago Jan Armstrong was ticking off the minutes, but not out of any particular safety concern; her concern was still the one she had expressed much earlier: would they be able to do all they had been assigned to do on this first lunar landing mission? Waiting for Buzz to come out, Joan Aldrin reacted to Armstrong's physical descriptions of the lunar surface with amazement. "He *likes* it!" Later Neil Armstrong said. . . .

"The most dramatic recollections I had were the sights themselves. Of all the spectacular views we had, the most impressive to me was on the way to the moon, when we flew through its shadow. We were still thousands of miles away, but close enough so that the moon almost filled our circular window. It was eclipsing the sun, from our position, and the corona of the sun was visible around the limb of the moon as a gigantic lens-shaped or saucer-shaped light, stretching out to several lunar diameters. It was magnificent, but the moon was even more so. We were in its shadow, so there was no part of it illuminated by the sun. It was illuminated only by earthshine. It made the moon appear blue-grey, and the entire scene looked decidedly three-dimensional.

"I was really aware, visually aware, that the moon was in fact a sphere, not a disc. It seemed almost as if it were showing us its roundness, its similarity in shape to our earth, in a sort of welcome. I was sure that it would be a hospitable host. It had been awaiting its first visitors for a long time."

A FAMILY IN HIDING

ANNE FRANK

from The Diary of Anne Frank

Anne Frank was a German Jewish girl, the daughter of a Frankfurt businessman. When the Nazis came to power, Anne's family moved to Amsterdam to escape persecution, but when Holland was invaded in 1941, they were in danger again. The family went into hiding in a sealed office in a warehouse in July 1942 and remained there for over two years. Anne kept her diary throughout this time. In August 1944, they were discovered and sent to concentration camps. Only Anne's father survived. He later retrieved and published Anne's diary. This episode tells how burglars tried to break into the warehouse one night.

Tuesday, April 11, 1944

D EAR KITTY,
My head throbs, I honestly don't know where to begin.

On Friday (Good Friday) we played Monopoly, Saturday afternoon too. These days passed quickly and uneventfully. On Sunday afternoon, on my invitation, Peter came to my room at half-past four; at a quarter-past five we went to the front attic, where we remained until six o'clock. There was a beautiful Mozart concert on the radio from six o'clock until a quarter-past seven. I enjoyed it all very much, but especially the *Kleine Nachtmusik*. I can hardly listen in the room because I'm always so inwardly stirred when I hear lovely music.

On Sunday evening Peter and I went to the front attic together and, in order to sit comfortably, we took with us a few divan cushions that we were able to lay our hands on. We seated ourselves on one packing-case. Both the case and the cushions were very narrow, so we sat absolutely squashed together, leaning against other cases. Mouschi kept us company too, so we weren't unchaperoned.

Suddenly, at a quarter to nine, Mr Van Daan whistled and asked if we had one of Dussel's cushions. We both jumped up and went downstairs with cushion, cat and Van Daan.

A lot of trouble arose out of this cushion, because Dussel was annoyed that we had one of his cushions, one that he used as a pillow. He was afraid that there might be fleas in it and made a great commotion about his beloved cushion! Peter and I put two hard brushes in his bed as a revenge. We had a good laugh over this little interlude!

Our fun didn't last long. At half-past nine Peter knocked softly on the door and asked Daddy if he would just help him upstairs over a difficult English sentence. "That's a blind," I said to Margot, "anyone could see through that one!" I was right. They were in the act of breaking into the warehouse. Daddy, Van Daan, Dussel and Peter were downstairs in a flash. Margot, Mummy, Mrs Van Daan and I stayed upstairs and waited.

Four frightened women just have to talk, so talk we did, until we heard a bang downstairs. After that all was quiet, the clock struck a quarter to ten. The colour had vanished from our faces, we were still quiet, although we were afraid. Where could the men be? What was that bang?

Would they be fighting the burglars? Ten o'clock, footsteps on the stairs: Daddy, white and nervy, entered, followed by Mr Van Daan. "Lights out, creep upstairs, we expect the police in the house!"

There was no time to be frightened: the lights went out, I quickly grabbed a jacket and we were upstairs. "What has happened? Tell us quickly!" There was no one to tell us, the men having disappeared downstairs again. Only at ten past ten did they reappear; two kept watch at Peter's open window, the door to the landing was closed, the swinging bookcase shut. We hung a jersey round the night light, and after that they told us: Peter had heard two loud bangs on the landing, ran downstairs and saw there was a large plank out of the left half of the door. He dashed upstairs, warned the "Home Guard" of the family and the four of them proceeded downstairs. When they entered the warehouse, the burglars were in the act of enlarging the hole. Without further thought Van Daan shouted: "Police!"

A few hurried steps outside, and the burglars had fled. In order to avoid the hole being noticed by the police, a plank was put against it, but a good hard kick from outside sent it flying to the ground. The men were perplexed at such impudence, and both Van Daan and Peter felt murder welling up within them; Van Daan beat on the ground with a chopper, and all was quiet again. Once more they wanted to put the plank in front of the hole. Interruption! A married couple outside shone a torch through the opening, lighting up the whole warehouse. "Hell!" muttered one of the men, and now they switched over from their rôle of police to that of burglars. The four of them sneaked upstairs, Peter quickly opened the doors and windows of the kitchen and private office, flung the telephone on to the floor and finally the four of them landed behind the swinging bookcase. — End of Part One.

The married couple with the torch would probably have warned the police: it was Sunday evening, Easter Sunday, no one at the office on Easter Monday, so none of us could budge until Tuesday morning. Think of it, waiting in such fear for two nights and a day! No one had anything to suggest, so we simply sat there in pitch darkness, because Mrs Van Daan in her fright had unintentionally turned the lamp right out; talked in whispers, and at every creak one heard "Sh! sh!"

It turned half-past ten, eleven, but not a sound; Daddy and Van Daan joined us in turns. Then a quarter-past eleven, a bustle and noise downstairs. Everyone's breath was audible, otherwise no one moved. Footsteps in the house, in the private office, kitchen, then... on our staircase. No one breathed audibly now, footsteps on our staircase, then a rattling of the swinging bookcase. This moment is indescribable. "Now we are lost!" I said, and could see us all being taken away by the Gestapo that very night. Twice they rattled at the bookcase, then there was nothing, the footsteps withdrew, we were saved so far. A shiver seemed to pass from one to another, I heard someone's teeth chattering, no one said a word.

There was not another sound in the house, but a light was burning on our landing, right in front of the bookcase. Could that be because it was a secret bookcase? Perhaps the police had forgotten the light? Would someone come back to put it out? Tongues loosened, there was no one in the house any longer – but perhaps there was someone on guard outside.

Next we did three things: we went over again what we supposed had happened, we trembled with fear, and we had to go to the lavatory. The buckets were in the attic, so all we had was Peter's tin wastepaper basket. Van Daan went first, then Daddy, but Mummy was too shy to face it. Daddy brought the wastepaper basket into the room, where Margot, Mrs Van Daan and I gladly made use of it. Finally Mummy decided to do so too. People kept on asking for paper – fortunately I had some in my pocket!

The tin smelt ghastly, everything went on in a whisper, we were tired, it was twelve o'clock. "Lie down on the floor then and sleep." Margot and I were each given a pillow and one blanket; Margot lying just near the store-cupboard and I between the table legs. The smell wasn't quite so bad when one was on the floor, but still Mrs Van Daan quietly fetched some chlorine, a tea towel over the pot serving as a second expedient.

Talk, whispers, fear, stink, people breaking wind, and always someone on the pot; then try to go to sleep! However, by half-past two I was so tired that I knew no more until half-past three. I awoke when Mrs Van Daan laid her head on my foot.

"For Heaven's sake, give me something to put on!" I asked. I was given something, but don't ask what – a pair of woollen knickers over my pyjamas, a red jumper, and a black skirt, white over-socks and a pair of sports stockings full of holes. Then Mrs Van Daan sat in the chair and her

husband came and lay on my feet. I lay thinking till half-past three, shivering the whole time, which prevented Van Daan from sleeping. I prepared myself for the return of the police, then we'd have to say that we were in hiding; they would either be good Dutch people, then we'd be saved, or the N.S.B., [The Dutch National Socialist Movement] then we'd have to bribe them!

"In that case, destroy the radio," sighed Mrs Van Daan. "Yes, in the stove!" replied her husband. "If they find us, then let them find the radio as well!"

"Then they will find Anne's diary," added Daddy. "Burn it then," suggested the most terrified member of the party. This, and when the police rattled the cupboard door, were my worst moments. "Not my diary, if my diary goes, I go with it!" But luckily Daddy didn't answer.

There is no object in recounting all the conversations that I can still remember; so much was said. I comforted Mrs Van Daan, who was very scared. We talked about escaping and being questioned by the Gestapo, about ringing up, and being brave.

"We must behave like soldiers, Mrs Van Daan. If all is up now, then let's go for Queen and Country, for freedom, truth and right, as they always say on Radio Orange. The only thing that is really rotten is that we get a lot of other people into trouble too."

Mr Van Daan changed places again with his wife after an hour, and Daddy came and sat beside me. The men smoked non-stop, now and then there was a deep sigh, then someone went on the pot and everything began all over again.

Four o'clock, five o'clock, half-past five. Then I went and sat with Peter by his window and listened, so close together that we could feel each other's bodies quivering; we spoke a word or two now and then, and listened attentively. In the room next door they took down the black-out. They wanted to ring up Koophuis at seven o'clock and get him to send someone round. Then they wrote down everything they wanted to tell Koophuis over the phone. The risk that the police on guard at the door, or in the warehouse, might hear the telephone was very great, but the danger of the police returning was even greater.

The points were these:

Burglars broken in: police have been in the house, as far as the swinging bookcase, but no further.

Burglars apparently disturbed, forced open the door in the warehouse and escaped through the garden.

Main entrance bolted, Kraler must have used the second door when he left. The typewriters and adding machine are safe in the black case in the private office.

Try to warn Henk and fetch the key from Elli, then go and look round the office – on the pretext of feeding the cat.

Everything went according to plan, Koophuis was rung up, the typewriters which we had upstairs were put in the case. Then we sat round the table again and waited for Henk or the police.

Peter had fallen asleep and Van Daan and I were lying on the floor, when we heard loud footsteps downstairs. I got up quietly: "That's Henk."

"No, no, it's the police," some of the others said.

Someone knocked at the door, Miep whistled. This was too much for Mrs Van Daan, she turned as white as a sheet and sank limply into a chair; had the tension lasted one minute longer she would have fainted.

Our room was a perfect picture when Miep and Henk entered, the table alone would have been worth photographing! A copy of *Cinema and Theatre*, covered with jam and a remedy for diarrhoea, opened at a page of dancing girls, two jam pots, two partly eaten pieces of bread, a mirror, comb, matches, ash, cigarettes, tobacco, ash-tray, books, a pair of pants, a torch, toilet paper, etc. etc., lay jumbled together in variegated splendour.

Of course Henk and Miep were greeted with shouts and tears. Henk mended the hole in the door with some planks, and soon went off again to inform the police of the burglary. Miep had also found a letter under the warehouse door from the night watchman Slagter, who had noticed the hole and warned the police, whom he would also visit.

So we had half an hour to tidy ourselves. I've never seen such a change take place in half an hour. Margot and I took the bedclothes downstairs, went to the W.C., washed and did our teeth and hair. After that I tidied the room a bit and went upstairs again. The table there was already cleared, so we ran off some water and made coffee and tea, boiled the milk and laid the table for lunch. Daddy and Peter emptied the potties and cleaned them with warm water and chlorine.

At eleven o'clock we sat round the table with Henk, who was back by that time, and slowly things began to be more normal and cosy again. Henk's story was as follows:

Mr Slagter was asleep, but his wife told Henk that her husband had found the hole in our door when he was

doing his tour round the canals, and that he had fetched a policeman, who had gone through the building with him. He would be coming to see Kraler on Tuesday and would tell him more then. At the police station they knew nothing of the burglary yet, but the policeman had made a note of it at once and would come and look round on Tuesday. On the way back Henk happened to meet our greengrocer at the corner, and told him that the house had been broken into. "I know that," he said quite coolly. "I was passing last evening with my wife and saw the hole in the door. My wife wanted to walk on, but I just had a look in with my torch; then the thieves cleared at once. To be on the safe side, I didn't ring up the police, as with you I didn't think it was the thing to do. I don't know anything, but I guess a lot."

Hank thanked him and went on. The man obviously guesses that we're here, because he always brings the potatoes during the lunch hour. Decent chap!

It was one by the time Henk had gone and we'd finished the washing-up. We all went for a sleep. I awoke at a quarter to three and saw that Mr Dussel had already disappeared. Quite by chance, and with my sleepy eyes, I ran into Peter in the bathroom; he had just come down. We arranged to meet downstairs.

I tidied myself and went down. "Do you still dare to go to the front attic?" he asked. I nodded, fetched my pillow and we went up to the attic. It was glorious weather, and soon the sirens were wailing; we stayed where we were. Peter put his arm round my shoulder, and I put mine round his and so we remained, our arms round each other, quietly waiting until Margot came to fetch us for coffee at four o'clock.

We finished our bread, drank lemonade and joked (we were able to again), and everything else went normally. In the evening I thanked Peter because he was the bravest of us all.

None of us has ever been in such danger as that night.

God truly protected us; just think of it – the police at our secret cupboard, the light on right in front of it, and still we remained undiscovered.

If the invasion comes, and bombs with it, then it is each man for himself, but in this case the fear was also for our good innocent protectors. "We are saved, go on saving us!" That is all we can say.

This affair has brought quite a number of changes with it. Mr Dussel no longer sits downstairs in Kraler's office in the evenings, but in the bathroom instead. Peter goes round the house for a check-up at half-past eight and half-past nine. Peter isn't allowed to have his window open at nights any more. No one is allowed to pull the plug after half-past nine. This evening there's a carpenter coming to make the warehouse doors even stronger.

Now there are debates going on all the time in the "Secret Annexe." Kraler reproached us for our carelessness. Henk, too, said that in a case like that we must never go downstairs. We have been pointedly reminded that we are in hiding, that we are Jews in chains, chained to one spot, without any rights, but with a thousand duties. We Jews mustn't show our feelings, must be brave and strong, must accept all inconveniences and not grumble, must do what is within our power and trust in God. Some time this terrible war will be over. Surely the time will come when we are people again, and not just Jews.

Who has inflicted this upon us? Who has made us Jews different to all other people? Who has allowed us to suffer so terribly up till now? It is God that has made us as we are, but it will be God, too, who will raise us up again. If we bear all this suffering and if there are still Jews left, when it is over, then Jews, instead of being doomed, will be held up as an example. Who knows, it might even be our religion from which the world and peoples learn good, and for that reason and that reason only, do we have to suffer now. We can never become just Netherlanders, or

just English, or representatives of any country for that matter, we will always remain Jews, but we want to, too.

Be brave! Let us remain aware of our task and not grumble, a solution will come, God has never deserted our people. Right through the ages there have been Jews, through all the ages they have had to suffer, but it has made them strong too; the weak fall, but the strong will remain and never go under!

During that night I really felt that I had to die, I waited for the police, I was prepared, as the soldier is on the battlefield. I was eager to lay down my life for the country, but now, now I've been saved again, now my first wish after the war is that I may become Dutch! I love the Dutch, I love this country, I love the language and want to work here. And even if I have to write to the Queen myself, I will not give up until I have reached my goal.

I am becoming still more independent of my parents, young as I am, I face life with more courage than Mummy;

my feeling for justice is immovable, and truer than hers. I know what I want, I have a goal, an opinion, I have a religion and love. Let me be myself and then I am satisfied. I know that I'm a woman, a woman with inward strength and plenty of courage.

If God lets me live, I shall attain more than Mummy ever has done, I shall not remain insignificant, I shall work in the world and for mankind.

And now I know that first and foremost I shall require courage and cheerfulness!

Yours, ANNE

FORGOTTEN

PEGGY SAY and PETER KNOBLER

Terry Anderson was chief Middle East correspondent for Associated Press when he was kidnapped in Beirut and became the longest-held American hostage in the Lebanon. His sister Peggy battled to save him for many years. Terry Anderson was eventually released on 4th December 1991. In this extract, Peggy learns from Father Jenco, another hostage who has been released, the conditions in which her brother is being held.

THE ASSOCIATED PRESS organized an afternoon in Joliet, Illinois, where the Jencos lived, for all of us to sit around with Father Jenco and talk to him at length, to find out what we could about Terry and about what it meant to be a hostage.

Father Jenco was good with details; after 564 days in captivity they were fresh in his mind. He told us that the hostages were permitted to wash and go to the bathroom only once a day. Other than that they had to use jars to hold their urine. In the beginning of his captivity, his captors made him balance his urine jar on his head and stand there until he fainted. The hostages used their left hands to wipe themselves because they had to have one hand clean to eat with. This was the way they lived.

Several times, when being transported, Father Jenco had been bound from head to foot with tape, with only his nose left uncovered. They then tied him into the wheel well of a truck and drove to their destination. But the roads in Lebanon are not all well paved. Once, they hit a rut and the bridge of his nose hit the bottom of the truck and started bleeding. His mouth was taped shut and he couldn't breathe. In his panic, blind and struggling, he had thought he was going to drown.

Father Jenco and Terry were unusually close. It was clear from the warmth of his conversation that he really liked my brother.

When Terry was first brought in, Father Jenco had been living in a closet in that room for several weeks. There was a crack in the closet door and Father Jenco said that as he dozed off and on in the closet, each time he woke up he would immediately peek through the crack to make sure Terry was still there. Even though they didn't know one another and were forbidden to speak, Father Jenco was comforted at the sight of another American. Later, when they were separated into cubicles they could hear when someone new had entered, and they could hear the tapping on the bathroom walls when each man was finished with his fifteen-minute ablutions. So the men knew they weren't alone, but nothing more.

Each of the hostages had been asking the captors to allow them to come together to hold a prayer service, and finally the guards relented. "We were brought into a room together, still blindfolded and still dragging our chains, and we were allowed to hug one another, but we weren't allowed to talk," said Father Jenco. "When we hugged, we whispered our names in one another's ears. And we had our prayer service."

Terry had asked to be allowed some privacy with Father Jenco to give his confession. The captors didn't understand what confession was, but they did let Terry and Father Jenco go into a room together. "When I pushed up my blindfold to see the face of this other human being, and Terry made his confession, at that moment we all believed we were going to die. And we were ready."

In their cubicles they could hear William Buckley pass toward death. The U.S. government contends, because it serves its own purposes to do so, that Buckley, the CIA station chief in Beirut, was tortured to death by his captors. Buckley may have been tortured earlier but Father Jenco maintained that Buckley was never tortured, period; he knew for a fact, he said, that Buckley died of pneumonia. They were in the same room with him and could hear him failing. In fact, Father Jenco said he heard Buckley say in the midst of his delirium, "I'd like poached eggs on toast, please."

Buckley wanted water and Father Jenco was begging the guards to give the man water. He and Terry were praying for Buckley. One night they heard what he said were the "obvious sounds of death." The guards came in and dragged Buckley out. That was the last they heard of him.

The guards became very frightened; they hadn't intended for Buckley to die. They brought in a doctor, a very compassionate Jewish doctor who was being held by the same captors with two other Jews, and made him examine the remaining hostages. Suddenly their living conditions improved.

They heard a short time later that all three Jewish hostages had been put to death.

Some time later all five hostages – Terry, Father Jenco, David Jacobsen, Tom Sutherland and Ben Weir – were put together. There were five men of extremely diverse personalities living day after day in an underground eight-by-ten concrete room.

Terry, said Father Jenco, was the one who found it most difficult to live without news. He was a newsman and it drove him crazy. One time he went on a hunger strike for three days to get a newspaper. "I said to Terry, 'They don't watch us eat anyway. Just *say* you are on a hunger strike.' But Terry said, 'No way,' he would not eat until they brought him a newspaper. So after three days they

gave him a newspaper. It was in Arabic."

"Ha, ha," the captors would say, "here's a story about you." And they would laugh. "We're not going to read it to you." Little cruelties. Father Jenco reminded us that these guards were kids, eighteen to twenty years old. Some were kind to them, some were unbearably cruel.

Terry would wrestle with one of the guards. Of course, he had to keep his blindfold on, and he was always very careful to lose; there was no telling what fate pinning your guard would bring you.

Looking for any means of diversion, Terry wove rosaries from fibres he pulled out of the mattress he slept on, and passed then out to the other hostages. He made chess pieces out of the tinfoil their cheese came in, until the captors took them away, saying that chess was forbidden in Islam.

He made playing cards out of the pages of books they

were given. The guards would confiscate them, but he would just make another set. "Terry was a vindictive hearts player," Father Jenco told me. "Nobody could beat him because he had a photographic memory. When Terry got out the cards and started looking for his victim we would all get very busy. Nobody wanted to play with him. But Terry would harass us so badly that somebody would finally sit down and play.

"One of our jokes was, when the guards would ask if there was anything they could get us, we would always yell, 'a taxi!'" When his captors pushed Father Jenco out of their car as he was being released, one of them threw several Lebanese pounds at him and snarled, "Call your taxi now!"

Terry and David Jacobsen, he said, fought constantly about politics. "Every time Terry got bored, we knew David was in trouble."

Every day the prisoners were taken out, one at a time, and allowed fifteen minutes to go to the bathroom, wash their clothes, wash themselves, their utensils. "That was the opportunity for the rest of us to talk about the one who was gone.

"Terry became the Felix Unger of the group. This is a guy who argued because he wanted to hem my pants. He mended everybody's clothing, he swept the place.

"Every once in a while they would give us pens. Terry would use up the ink out of everyone's pen. We had to hide them. He was always writing stuff down. For me, I'd get up in the morning, I'd go to the toilet, that is my day. I'm in captivity, what is there to write about? Not Terry. Scribble, scribble, scribble all the time.

"For the rest of us, when we were told to do something, even if it was bizarre or undignified, we did it; it wasn't worth the argument. Not Terry. He would never do anything he did not want to do. His attitude was, 'Beat me, kill me, whatever you want to do, but I'm not doing it.' "

They lived mostly in their underpants, Father Jenco said. "We called it our three-piece hostage suit: blindfold, chains, and underpants. Every once in a while the guards would come in and check our undershorts for contraband. Me, what do I care? Not Terry. No way were they going to look in his underpants. And they didn't. He was adamant about it."

"It was not so much surviving captivity," he laughed, "as surviving Terry Anderson. Our only hope was that every time Terry would get involved in a new project, he would drop it and move on to something else. About the worst one was when Terry took up jogging. Now, I love your brother dearly, but we were not allowed to shower. And we were in a very small space. Everybody complained because of the noise his feet made, slapping on the floor as he ran around the room. And you can imagine what he began to smell like.

"But, so as not to offend anybody, Terry got a pair of socks and sewed pads on the feet so when he ran around the room his feet wouldn't make any noise.

"He had been learning Arabic from Ben Weir, but then Ben got out. Tom Sutherland was the dean of agriculture [at the American University of Beirut], so Terry took an interest in farming. He would get a project in his head and build it. He and Tom built a farm, cow by cow, building by building. They calculated how many cows they needed, how much milk they produced, how much they needed to eat, how many acres per cow.

"When they finished the farm, Terry went on to a restaurant he was going to build. You were going to cook, Peggy."

"Father Jenco," I said, "not even for Terry Anderson would I go back to cooking."

"Whenever the guards gave us a book," he went on, "Terry would read it over and over again. He'd read that book all through the night. There would be Terry with his candle, because he never knew when they were going to snatch it from us. Of course, that left the rest of us with nothing to read."

They gave him a Mr T. puzzle and Terry worked until he got it down to the very minimum time that any human being could put that puzzle together. "He constantly sought diversion for his mind," said Father Jenco. "It was the hardest thing for him to contend with."

When Father Jenco had greeted me in Damascus he said, "I have a message to you from Terry's captors: They send condolences on the death of your father and brother." But they'd never told Terry. They did tell him, in Father Jenco's presence, something to the effect of "Boy, your sister really sticks it to the government."

Father Jenco is a gentle soul; he wants to believe that he turned these people around, that some of the guards loved him. One of the guards, a boy by the name of Said, was kind to him, even went so far as to bring him popcorn. Father Jenco said, "Peggy, you must forgive these people."

I said, "Excuse me, Father, but I don't call people compassionate who bring you popcorn one day and kick you in the stomach the next, I'm sorry, it doesn't compute with me. I'm not a priest, I don't have that kind of forgiveness in my heart."

RESCUE MISSION

ANTHONY MASTERS

S IX MILLION JEWISH MEN, women and children were killed by the Nazis during the Second World War – exterminated systematically in a way which nowadays would be called ethnic cleansing. By 1944 a million of these Jews were trapped in Hungary, which had become a sanctuary for European Jewry. Their safety was short-lived. That summer, Nazi troops entered Hungary and with them what was known as Eichmann's Death Machine – a military corps that was dedicated to removing these Jews to the camps and the deadly gas chambers of World War II.

A group of young Jewish *émigrés* living in Palestine – soon to become the state of Israel – were deeply concerned at the fate of their people and formed a plan to rescue them. Their aim was to parachute back into Europe and open up escape routes for the vulnerable and isolated Jews, but the parachutists were ludicrously low in numbers. The original plan had been to drop hundreds of Jewish parachutists behind the lines, but in the end only thirty-two jumped and, of these, six young people parachuted into Hungary – five men and a girl. None of them was over twenty-five.

229

Hannah Senesh, the only girl in the group, emigrated to Palestine from Hungary in 1939 when she was eighteen. An intellectual and a Zionist – someone who believed that a Jewish homeland could be created in Palestine – her sense of personal mission had developed at an early age during a privileged childhood in Hungary. The diaries that Hannah wrote at agricultural school in Palestine and later on at her kibbutz, clearly indicate her fears for the European Jews, but even she never realised the full extent of the carnage.

Hannah was a person of strong beliefs and considerable fortitude. Conditions in her kibbutz at Haifa were grim – as an excerpt from her diary shows:

I'll try to write a bit, though my hands are nearly frozen. Outside – a fearful storm. Five tents were blown down during the night. Ours didn't collapse, but the wind is howling around it on all sides, sand has covered everything, and my bed is rocking ceaselessly with a monotonous beat.

Today is my Sabbath, my day off. I've wrapped one rag on top of another around myself, and am now in one of the rooms, since it's impossible to remain in the tent. I want to write about the past year. Without noticing, we stepped into 1942.

It is a grey, rainy day that depresses one's very soul, and though the rain doesn't penetrate the room, it robs me of the incentive to do anything.

It's difficult to believe this grey, dismal rain will ever stop – and the same applies to the war. It doesn't touch us, yet locks us in our rooms, denies us our peace of mind – though we do not suffer from it the way the peoples of Europe are suffering. It's hard to imagine that spring and sunshine will come again, and difficult even in this little house to do anything, to clean it, pretty it up a bit. One just doesn't have the desire to do anything. It's possible that the rain will come in, that there may be leaks. But who wants to go out in the pouring rain to build, to mend, to do?

Her self-sacrificing attitude to the rigours of the course she had chosen was already preparing her for a single-minded act of considerable courage, and her belief in her people was unswerving, despite the fact that it was not taken seriously even by her fellow kibbutzniks. She confided to her diary:

Here in the settlement I think I've reached the second phase. It's hard to explain the basis for my feelings, but I sense a coldness, and a lack of trust. The cause is obvious: either they think I'm very naive, or take me for a chatterbox who arrogantly talks big about things she can never realise. They think my initial enthusiasm and activity will wane as I encounter reality. Naturally, no one has said any of this to me, but I'm sensitive enough to feel it. How shall I react to all this? I've decided to be careful what I say, and to do nothing. Eventually people will get to know me as I am, and will judge me accordingly – neither for better nor for worse.

Sometimes I ask myself whether I care what the people here think of me. But what is of paramount importance is that my estimate of myself be clear. As far as I'm concerned, I really know all my faults and inadequacies. Of course I'd be lying if I said I was not aware of my good traits as well.

Today I washed 150 pairs of socks. I thought I'd go mad.

In January 1943, Hannah decided to return to Hungary, however high the odds that were stacked against her.

I've had a shattering week. I was suddenly struck by the idea of going to Hungary. I feel I must be there during these days in order to help organise youth immigration, and also to bring my mother out. Although I'm quite aware how absurd the idea is, it still seems both feasible and necessary to me, so I'll get to work on it and carry it through. For the time being this is but a sudden enthusiasm, a hopeful plan to get Mother out and bring her here, at any cost.

In February, she was approached at her kibbutz by a man called Yonah Rosen, who was a Hungarian himself and a member of the Palmach, the striking force of the Haganah, the Palestinian Jewish Self Reliance Army. Hannah's sense of mission was immediately fulfilled when Rosen told her that there was to be a Palestinian Jewish parachute mission to Europe. The plan was that groups of Jewish parachutists were to be dropped behind the lines in Europe. Separate units would be formed, and to avoid arousing suspicion each unit would only consist of nationals of that particular country. The operation would be assisted by the British who would provide training, equipment and planes. In return for their involvement, the British wanted the parachutists' first priority to be the provision of escape routes for Allied airmen shot down behind the lines or those trying to escape from prisoner of war camps. The parachutists were to work with local partisans. After they had completed these tasks they were then free to help their own people – a very basic compromise indeed. Nevertheless, Rosen recommended acceptance of the terms, as clearly, if they were not agreed to, then there would be no possibility of the mission taking place. Nevertheless, the suicidal nature of the operation was beginning to make itself all too clear.

Hannah wrote in her diary:

My answer, of course, was that I'm absolutely ready. It's still only in the planning stage, but he promised to bring the matter up before the enlistment committee since he considers me admirably suited for the mission.

I see the hand of destiny in this just as I did at the time of my aliya [immigration to the Holy Land]. I wasn't master of my fate then either. I was enthralled by one idea, and it gave me no rest. I knew I would immigrate, despite the many obstacles in my path. Now I again sense the excitement of something important and vital ahead, and the feeling of inevitability connected with a decisive and urgent step. The entire plan may miscarry, and I may receive a brief notification informing me the matter will be postponed, or that I don't qualify. But I think I have the capabilities necessary for just this assignment, and I'll fight for it with all my might.

I can't sleep at night because of the scenes I envisage: how I'll conduct myself in this or that situation. . . how I'll notify Mother of my arrival. . . how I'll organise the Jewish youth. Everything is still indefinite. We'll see what the future brings. . .

After a long delay Hannah was interviewed by a joint panel of British and Jewish personnel and, in the winter of 1943, went into training at an outlying kibbutz. The mission was to be under British command, and its members would eventually be British officers; final training was to take place in Egypt.

Hannah's single-mindedness in her approach to the mission was underlined by a fellow parachutist, Yoel Palgi:

Hannah was the chief rebel. And she was not always right. On the contrary. More often than not, she was wrong. At the same time I could not even distinguish between her tense impatience, and dedication to our mission – which to her was the only thing that mattered. She was totally unconcerned about her own safety.

Sometimes I wondered how I would ever be able to work with her once we were in enemy territory. She didn't appear to be sufficiently co-operative, she seemed concerned only with her own goals; she was totally lacking in caution, and refused to accept discipline. She insisted that we divide up the fields of activity in advance, so we would not have to waste time on such matters once we were dropped. She wanted to be sure she got her share of the action, that she would not be left out.

After the jump into Yugoslavia, the parachutists stayed with partisans where Palgi records:

Her eyes no longer sparkled. She was cold, sharp, her reasoning now razor-edged; she no longer trusted strangers. She was the first to suspect the partisans of unwillingness to help and of misleading us. We argued with her about this, but she was adamant, and finally succeeded in making us suspicious as well. Only weeks later it became clear how right she had been, and that we were, in truth, being completely misled by the partisans. They regarded us as allies, but they didn't trust anyone – including their allies. And if Hannah was difficult to get along with before, she was ten times more so now. At first she had only sensed the forces that lay dormant within her; but now she was fully conscious of them and had unlimited faith in herself.

Just what brought about this change in Hannah is difficult to say – perhaps the German occupation of Hungary or being so often under enemy fire, but whatever the reason her missionary feeling intensified. She was impatient, unwilling to listen to suggestions that she should delay crossing the border – no matter how sound and reasonable the advice. She had her own theory: "We are the only ones who can possibly help, we don't have the right to think of our own safety; we don't have the right to hesitate. Even if the chances of our success are minuscule, we must go. If we don't go for fear of our lives, a million Jews will surely be massacred. If we succeed, our work can open great and important avenues of activity. Thanks to our efforts, multitudes will be saved."

I felt that she was wrong and that if we crossed into enemy territory and failed, we would end the entire action – as had happened in other lands. But it was impossible to oppose her. She turned against anyone who disagreed with her point of view. I told her I thought she was wrong, but that I was not going to fight over it, even though her decision made my departure mandatory.

After a frustrating period of inaction with Hannah desperate to cross the border, she was at last allowed to enter Hungary with three colleagues. They had to swim the rain-swollen, swirling currents of the river Drava. Unfortunately, two of them were routinely searched in a nearby village which resulted in one of them committing suicide – thus signing Hannah's death warrant. After

hiding in reed beds for some hours, she and her remaining colleague buried their transmitter and guns in a small wood. Soon, they realised it was being surrounded by German soldiers and desperately posed as lovers. Nevertheless they were arrested and the woods were searched thoroughly. Eventually the transmitter was found.

Under heavy guard, Hannah was put on a train to her home city of Budapest – the place from which she had so optimistically hoped to rescue as many Jews as possible. In an attempt to force Hannah to reveal her transmitter code, the journey was preceded by systematic beatings. Knowing that she was coming to breaking point, Hannah opened the door of the speeding train and tried to throw herself out, but her guard grabbed her before it was too late, commenting, "You are state property. We'll do away with you when we no longer need you."

Hannah ended up with some satisfaction at least. The

book of French poems she had been allowed to take with her to Budapest in fact contained her transmitter code and, quite purposefully, she left it on the train. Now, whatever the Germans did to her, she would not be able to give away the information.

She was taken from Budapest railway station to Horthy Miklos Street Military Prison and tortured, but Hannah refused to give anything away but her name and number. As the tormented day inched slowly by, her torturers beat her on the palms of the hand and on the soles of her feet. She was also stripped and beaten, her hair was pulled out in fistfuls, a tooth was knocked out and she was flogged for hours in a sitting position.

Eventually her mother, Catherine, still living in Budapest, was taken to see Hannah. Her first reaction was:

I felt as if the floor were giving away under me and clutched the edge of the table frantically with both hands. My eyes closed, and in a matter of seconds I felt everything – hope, faith, trust, the very meaning of life, everything I had ever believed in – collapse like a child's house of cards. I was completely shattered, physically and spiritually.

The door opened. I turned, my back to the table, my body rigid.

Four men led her in. Had I not known she was coming, perhaps in that first moment I would not have recognised the Hannah of five years ago. Her once soft wavy hair hung in a filthy tangle, her ravaged face reflected untold suffering, her large, expressive eyes were blackened, and there were ugly welts on her cheeks and neck. That was my first glimpse of her.

Ironically, Catherine was already preparing to escape to Palestine with some friends, but now that Hannah had been arrested she felt that she must stay. Shortly afterwards, she, too, was arrested by the Gestapo. Eventually, she was transferred to the same prison as Hannah and in fact could see her daughter through a cell-window just across the exercise yard. They established contact by writing the outline of letters in the air.

On the morning of September 11th, 1944, Catherine was

told by a trusty that Hannah had been taken to an undisclosed place. In fact this was the Conti Street Prison. Fellow-prisoner Palgi, bound for separate incarceration, said goodbye at the gates. He recalls that as his van drove off, Hannah put down her bag of minimal possessions and gave him a thumbs-up sign. That was the last time he saw her.

On October 28th, Hannah Senesh was tried for treason. She pleaded guilty and was granted permission to speak:

Hannah: "I do not admit treason to my native land, Hungary. I came here in the service of my Homeland, Eretz Israel. True, I was born in Budapest. Here I learned to love the beautiful, to honour my neighbour and to respect the good. The Hungarians were a beaten and suffering people. Through my love for them I learned to understand the beaten and the suffering. I dreamed of a beautiful world which would be compassionate towards Hungarians because of their suffering. I thought we would be able to repay the world for its compassion with what we had learned: an understanding for all the suffering

people of the world, and a desire to help the weak. My father was a Hungarian author who left an inheritance to me and to others: he taught us to have faith in the good. He set an example of working for the sake of goodness. Hungary was my first Homeland, and for a long time I thought that the spiritual Hungary I had absorbed from great Hungarian authors was the true Hungary. But when I grew up the streets of the city taught me that as a Jewess I had no place in this country. One by one, the politicians voted for race discrimination, deprivation of human rights, the cruelty of the Middle Ages. Farmers in the villages were hungry for bread and threatened the land-owners who, instead of dividing their surplus crops, threw them the Jews, history's scapegoat. I awakened from my dream, the dream of my father and my father's father. I understood then that I have no Homeland. You cancelled my citizenship with your hate. I went away to build a Homeland, a Homeland of my own, a Jewish Homeland, a true Homeland. The war came. And this regime, which had deluded the people for an entire generation, brought upon them the worst catastrophe. Unnecessarily, without justification, it dragged Hungary into the war – and on the wrong side. The side of evil."

(Shouted interruptions.)

President of the Tribunal: "Let her speak."

Hannah: "You paid for that deed, with the lives of hundreds of thousands of victims. To what end? To serve the traitorous generals of German sympathies who reigned in Hungary. You joined forces with our blood enemies – the Germans. And thus you became my enemy. But even that was not enough for me to come and fight against you. I still clung to the love of my youth. I was sorry for the Hungarian people who were always so close to my heart, who had fallen victim of their conscienceless leaders. And that was still not enough for you. You also raised your hand against my people. Thus it is not I who is the traitor! They are the traitors who brought this calamity upon our

239

people, and upon themselves! I implore you, don't add to your crimes. Save my people in the short time it remains in your power to do so. Every Jew who remains alive in Hungary will make the judgment against you after you fall!"

On November 7th she was sentenced to death and given an hour to prepare herself. After she had written some letters, a Captain appeared with two soldiers who took her to a yard inside the prison. There she was strapped to a wooden post. She refused a blindfold and calmly watched the procedure of the firing squad until a hail of bullets entered her body.

A MEDICAL REVOLUTION

from Louis Pasteur

Louis Pasteur (1822-1895) was a French scientist who taught chemistry at the university of Dijon and later became professor of science in Paris. His researches into bacteria led to great advances in the treatment of disease, especially with the invention of the vaccination process.

I T WAS JULY 6, 1885, when Louis Pasteur, looking up from his microscope, saw nine-year-old Joseph Meister come limping into his laboratory in Paris. Joseph was with his mother and a neighbour, Monsieur Vone. The three had left their little French village near the Swiss border and started for the city of Paris in search of the one man who might save the life of young Joseph.

Pasteur loved children, and the heart of this great scientist filled with horror when he learned that two days previously Joseph had been furiously attacked by a mad dog. The boy's hands, arms, and legs were badly bitten. The cuts in one arm were very deep. All in all, there were fourteen ugly wounds.

It had happened at eight o'clock in the morning when Joseph was on his way to school in the village of Meissengott in Alsace. The dog jumped on him and threw

him to the ground. A nearby bricklayer ran to his rescue and with an iron bar beat off the dog, which ran home only to bite its master, M. Vone, who grabbed a gun and shot it dead.

When the bricklayer picked Joseph up, he found him bleeding and covered with saliva from the dog. Examination of the contents of the dead dog's stomach showed that it was filled with hay, straw, and sticks of wood. The dog had been biting anything and everything it met as it madly tore about. There was no doubt about it, this angry dog had *rabies* – a deadly disease found among wild animals, especially wolves. Animals with this disease are called *rabid*, and the dog that attacked Joseph had sometime previously been bitten by a rabid animal.

For centuries the people of Alsace had lived in dread of mad wolves that strayed down from the Jura mountains and attacked dogs and human beings, spreading the disease among their victims. To be bitten by a rabid animal was almost always fatal. Joseph's parents were terrified. It did not seem possible that their son could live.

That evening, twelve hours after the accident, they had taken him to a country doctor, Dr Weber, who burned Joseph's wounds with Carbolic Acid. He urged them to take him at once to Paris – a two-day journey. There they must find and consult Louis Pasteur who, although not a physician, would know more than anyone else whether there was any chance of saving their son.

"Pasteur has saved dogs from rabies," said Dr Weber. "Perhaps he can save Joseph." Joseph and his mother, accompanied by M. Vone, started at once on the long journey.

Pasteur was deeply moved at the sight of these three strangers: the frightened and suffering young boy, his grief-stricken mother, and the anxious and bewildered M. Vone. He carefully examined the man and soon assured him that he need have no concern about himself, for his coat sleeve had been heavy enough to protect his skin against the dog's teeth when it had grabbed his arm. Since his skin showed not even the slightest scratch, the rabies virus in the dog's saliva could not possibly have entered his system. Pasteur assured him that he could safely return home. Relieved but with a heavy heart, he went back to Meissengott, knowing that Joseph's life hung in the balance.

Pasteur turned to examine the young boy. The kindly face of this great scientist was sad and grave, for he knew that he must quickly make a serious and most difficult decision. What should he do for this boy? Did he dare to risk using the preventive rabies vaccine that he had successfully used on dogs? He had never tried his treatment on a human being. But he was sure of his experiments with dogs, because he had repeated them many times during the past four years.

First he had vaccinated healthy dogs against rabies by using material from the spinal cord of rabbits that had been injected with the rabies virus. The treatment consisted in giving dogs a series of twelve or more daily injections of emulsions of dried spinal cords of rabid rabbits. Such cords, dried for fourteen days, were so changed that emulsions of them were harmless, and yet they possessed the ability to stimulate the body of healthy dogs to make protective substances against the deadly virus. A cord dried thirteen days contained slightly stronger yet still harmless material. Daily injections of cords which had been dried for shorter and shorter periods were given until the treated animal actually resisted a final injection of the deadly virus itself. In fact, dogs treated in this way did not succumb to the disease even when bitten by a rabid dog. Pasteur knew that he could vaccinate dogs and protect them against rabies.

Even more important, he had recently saved the lives of dogs *after* they had been bitten, by giving them the same treatment. In all his experiments he had used over one hundred dogs, and he was very sure of his results. But he was not a physician and therefore had no legal right to treat a human being. Then, too, no one could be absolutely sure how the human body would respond to these injections. He must first consult Professor Vulpian, a physiologist, and Dr Grancher, a physician, who were both scientists familiar with his work. He hurried off to see them, for there was no time to waste.

The experts whom Pasteur consulted were of one opinion: Joseph *must* be given the Pasteur treatment against rabies. There was no other choice. If only the boy had been taken at once to the blacksmith's shop and had had his wounds cauterized by a red-hot iron, he might have had some slight chance of recovering. But there were fourteen wounds, some very deep, and they had been treated with carbolic acid twelve hours after the accident. The skin was broken in too many places, and the carbolic treatment had been used too late to give protection. His case was considered hopeless unless something drastic could be done. Pasteur's vaccine had saved the life of dogs. It might save the life of Joseph Meister. The first of the long series of daily injections was begun that night, almost sixty hours after the accident.

It was agreed, for two reasons, that Dr Grancher should give the injections. First, Pasteur's left hand was paralyzed from a stroke suffered when he was only forty-six years old, and it would have been difficult for him to handle the Pravaz syringe. Most important of all, however, he was not a physician and had no wish to treat Joseph illegally.

Pasteur arranged for the lodgings of Joseph and his mother at Rollin Collège, in Paris, and anxiously watched over the boy day and night. With great care, he directed the preparation of each dose. He was always present when the injections were given, making detailed notes of every step of the treatment.

As the days passed, Joseph's wounds grew less painful, and he learned not to dread the puncture of the needle when it was placed just under the skin of the abdomen. Joseph soon became very fond of the elderly man who took such an interest in him, who was so kind and gentle, and who even let him play with the guinea pigs in the laboratory cages.

But as the treatment continued, Pasteur was tormented with the fear that the boy might not survive in spite of his seeming good health, because the scientist knew only too well that the symptoms of rabies sometimes suddenly appear many weeks after the victim is bitten. On July 11th, five days after the first injection, Pasteur wrote to his son-in-law:

All is going well, the child sleeps well, has a good appetite, and the inoculated matter is absorbed into the system from one day to another without leaving a trace. It is true that I have not yet come to the test inoculations, which will take place Tuesday, Wednesday and Thursday. If the lad keeps well during the following weeks, I think the experiment will be sure to succeed.

Each inoculation was stronger than the previous one, and as the end of the treatment approached, Pasteur's anxiety increased. Mme Pasteur wrote to their children: "Your father has had another bad night; yet there can be no turning back now! The boy continues in perfect health."

The series of vaccinations lasted ten days, and Joseph received twelve shots. On July 16th, at 11 a.m. he had his last injection. When Joseph went to bed that night, he threw his arms around "Dear Monsieur Pasteur," as he had come to call him. While Joseph slept soundly, Pasteur spent a wretched night dreaming that the boy might die from the final, most powerful injection. But Joseph lived!

Pasteur, exhausted from so many days of mental anguish, left Paris for a short rest in the quiet country estate of his son-in-law in Burgundy. Joseph remained in Paris for several days under the watchful care of Dr Grancher, who kept Pasteur informed of the boy's health. But Pasteur could not calm down, and each morning anxiously waited reports from Paris. The news continued good.

By the end of July, Pasteur went as usual with Mme Pasteur to spend the summer in his boyhood home in the

town of Arbois. He refused to form hasty conclusions on the result of Joseph's treatment, but as the summer passed and Joseph remained well, his doubts vanished. By October, he was ready to report to the Academy of Sciences in Paris on his "Method of Preventing Rabies after a Bite." He announced:

After I might say innumerable experiments, I have arrived at a preventive method, practical and prompt, the success of which has been so convincing in dogs that I have confidence in its general application in all animals and even in man.

After describing the details of the treatment of Joseph Meister, Pasteur concluded: "Today, three months and three weeks after the accident, his health leaves nothing to be desired." He then went on to tell of the second lad who had just come to him for treatment.

On October 14th, six young peasant boys were watching their sheep in a meadow at the foot of the Jura mountains when suddenly they spied a large dog. Its jaw was hanging open and the animal was frothing at the mouth.

"A mad dog!" they cried out. Seeing the children, the dog dashed across the meadow, and the children ran shrieking in all directions. The oldest, Jean Jupille, armed with a whip, fought the infuriated animal in order to protect the escape of the younger shepherds. The dog seized his left hand between its jaws. Jean wrestled with it, threw it to the ground, and tried to free his hand. While doing so, the dog savagely bit his right hand. Finally, Jean wound the whip around the dog's jaws, grabbed his wooden shoe, and beat the animal over the head. To make sure it was dead, he dragged it to a nearby stream and held its head under water. With both hands bleeding, Jean returned to the village.

His wounds were bandaged, and the dog's body was recovered. The next day two veterinary surgeons declared that without doubt the dog had been rabid. The mayor of the village wrote to Pasteur giving him the whole story. Unless Jean Jupille could be vaccinated, the brave shepherd would die as a result of his own courage. Surely Pasteur could save him.

Pasteur answered immediately. He said that he had saved dogs bitten by a rabid dog if treatment was begun as late as six or even eight days after the biting. There was no time to waste, but Jean's parents must first consent to the treatment.

Jean started at once for Paris, but by the time he arrived six days had passed since the accident. The interval in the case of Joseph Meister had been only two and one-half days. Had too much time been lost to save young Jupille?

Pasteur had reason to be worried, for he was not certain he could save Jean's life. Yet his success with little Joseph gave him courage. He started Jean at once on his series of daily injections, but was constantly worried for fear something might go wrong. The boy's health remained good, the lapse of six days had not been too long. The boy's life was saved. The injections had had time to stimulate the body to produce protective substances which destroyed the viruses before they could reach the brain. Once they were in the brain, no known treatment could have saved him.

In 1885 people were sceptical about new medical discoveries – doctors more than patients. So it was inevitable that some day a person would go to Pasteur after a lapse of more than six days from the time of being bitten. Within a few weeks, Pasteur had to face just such a problem when Louise Pelletier was brought to him.

When he saw this little ten-year-old girl, he was filled with terror, for she had been severely bitten in the head thirty-three days earlier. The ugly wound was still an open sore. "This is a hopeless case," he thought to himself. "Rabies will no doubt appear at any moment. Whatever shall I do? If I treat her and she dies, people will say my method has failed. As a result, many bitten persons, discouraged from coming to the laboratory, will die of the disease. Shall I protect my method or fight a losing battle to save this little girl?" As these thoughts rushed through his mind, his compassion for the child and her parents, who begged him to try to save her, left him no choice.

Louise Pelletier completed the vaccine treatment and returned to school, but soon word came that she was dying. Pasteur rushed to her bedside, hoping that additional injections might yet save her. But it soon became evident that she would not live. She begged him not to leave her, nor could Pasteur bear to tear himself away. When all hope was gone, Pasteur turned to the parents and said, "I did so wish I could have saved your little one." As he left the house, he burst into tears.

As the months passed, news of the Pasteur treatment gradually spread far and wide, and hundreds of persons bitten by rabid dogs went to Paris for help. Nineteen Russians, one of them a priest who had been attacked by a wild wolf, reached Pasteur in serious condition. Sixteen of them survived.

As the number of persons receiving the rabies treatment

increased, so naturally, for one reason or another, did the failures. During the year following the treatment of Joseph Meister, 1,726 French persons bitten by mad dogs were vaccinated, and all but ten of them lived. Some physicians, unable to accept such a revolutionary idea as treatment with a vaccine prepared by a mere chemist, made the most of every failure: they accused Pasteur of murder, claiming his treatment had caused the death of Louise Pelletier.

His friend and supporter, Dr Grancher, described the rising feeling of hostility: "One day, I was at the Medical School for an examination... I heard a furious voice shouting, 'Yes, Pasteur is an assassin!' I walked in and saw a group of colleagues, who dispersed in silence."

At another time when supporting Pasteur against false accusations, Dr Grancher said: "The medical men who have been chosen by M. Pasteur to assist him in his work have not hesitated to practise the anti-rabic inoculation on themselves, as a safeguard against an accidental inoculation of the virus which they are constantly handling. What greater proof can they give of their bona fide convictions?"

Although Pasteur knew that most medical men in Paris

supported him, he was saddened by the bitterness of many angry debates. He received unsigned letters filled with false accusations. Insulting newspaper articles came off the presses, and mournfully he exclaimed, "I did not know I had so many enemies."

Some of his opponents were those who found it impossible to accept such a revolutionary idea as injecting into the human body a deadly rabies virus – no matter how weakened it might be. Even some of his own disciples wondered if enough work had been done on dogs to warrant its use in man. Some people even opposed experimenting with animals. Probably some of his enemies were those who still fought against the idea that microbes could cause disease, even though Pasteur had given convincing evidence to support this theory. And there were those who, always on the alert for slander, joined the forces of the opposition and gave support to smear campaigns.

Whenever Pasteur's adversaries attacked his work because of prejudice, without scientific evidence to support their criticisms, he lost his temper, his gentleness vanished, and in an aggressive manner he fought for the truth as he saw it. In this way he often antagonised others by the mere force and brilliance of his intellectual vigour. He had an unwavering confidence in himself whenever he was forced to fight ignorance, superstition, or prejudice.

To his great satisfaction and peace of mind, a commission of experts was appointed by the British government to repeat his work. Its members confirmed his experiments on dogs, and went to Paris to examine his clinical records of human cases. They even made detailed inquiries in the homes of ninety patients who had received the anti-rabies treatment. They finally concluded:

From the evidence of all these facts, we think it certain that the inoculations practised by M. Pasteur on persons bitten by rabid animals have prevented the occurrence of hydrophobia [rabies] in a

large proportion of those who, if they had not been so inoculated, would have died of that disease.

Even more important than Pasteur's contribution to the control of rabies was the fact that he established the idea that men, women, and little children could be protected against various diseases by vaccination – by injections of the weakened or dead microbe that caused the disease.

Over one hundred years before the days of Pasteur, Jenner had vaccinated people in England against smallpox. But Jenner had not *made* his vaccine. He had protected people against smallpox by injecting the fluid from sores on the hands of milkmaids afflicted with cowpox. Furthermore, Jenner had no theory to explain how his vaccine worked, and therefore the practice could not be applied to other diseases. Pasteur supported his own

practice by well-founded theories, and was the first to discover that vaccines can be *made*. It was Pasteur who prepared the way for other men to make vaccines for other diseases.

Pasteur lived for ten years after saving the life of Joseph Meister, long enough to see erected in Paris the great Pasteur Institute which has served as a clinic for rabies treatment and as a research centre for the study of other diseases caused by microbes. He rejoiced in knowing that the money which made this building possible came pouring in from French citizens, rich and poor alike: from contributions from his own government, from the Tsar of Russia, and Emperor Pedro II of Brazil. His pride rose when he read the name of Joseph Meister among the long list of individual donors who had contributed whatever they could.

Acknowledgements

The publisher would like to thank the copyright holders for permission to reproduce the following copyright material:

Excerpts from *Autobiography of Values* by Charles A. Lindbergh, copyright © 1978 by Harcourt Brace & Company and Anne Morrow Lindbergh, reprinted by permission of the publisher. Excerpt from *Mother Teresa: Sister to the Poor* by Patricia Reilly Giff, copyright © 1986 by Patricia Reilly Giff, reprinted by permission of Penguin Books USA Inc. Excerpt from *I Chose to Climb* by Chris Bonington, reprinted by permission of Victor Gollancz. Excerpt from *Black Foremothers: Three Lives* by Dorothy Sterling, copyright © 1988 by The Feminist Press at The City University of New York, reprinted by permission of the publisher. Excerpt from *The Small Woman* by Alan Burgess, reprinted by permission of Evans Brothers Ltd. Excerpt from *My Left Foot* by Christy Brown, published by Martin Secker & Warburg Ltd, reprinted by permission of the publisher. Excerpt from *The Struggle is My Life* by Nelson Mandela, published by IDAF Publications 1990, reprinted by permission of Mayibuye Centre, University of the Western Cape. Excerpt from *Children of the Siege* by Pauline Cutting, published by Heinemann 1988, reprinted by permission of Xandra Hardie. Excerpt from *A Testament of Hope: The Essential Writings of Martin Luther King, Jr.* edited by James Melvin Washington, published by Harper & Row 1986, reprinted by arrangement with The Heirs to the Estate of Martin Luther King, Jr., c/o Joan Daves Agency as agent for the proprietor. Copyright 1958 by Martin Luther King, Jr., copyright renewed 1986 by Coretta Scott King. Excerpts from *Woman in the Mists* by Farley Mowat, copyright © 1987 by Farley Mowat, reprinted by permission of Warner Books, New York. Excerpt from *Colditz* by Major P. R. Reid, published by Macmillan London Ltd 1984, reprinted by permission of the publisher. Excerpt from *Edison: The Man Who Made the Future* by Ronald W. Clark (pp9-16), (Rainbird, 1977), copyright © 1977 Ronald W. Clark, reprinted by permission of Penguin Books Ltd. Excerpts from *Come Hell or High Water* by Clare Francis, reprinted by permission of John Johnson Ltd. Excerpt from *Marie Curie* by Angela Bull, reprinted by permission of Evans Brothers Ltd. Excerpt from *Brunel and his World* by John Pudney, reprinted by permission of Thames and Hudson Ltd. Excerpts from *First on the Moon: A Voyage with Neil Armstrong, Michael Collins, Edwin E. Aldrin, Jr.* written with Gene Farmer and Dora Jane Hambling, reprinted by permission of Penguin Books Ltd. Excerpt from *The Diary of Anne Frank* by Anne Frank, translated by B. M. Mooyaart-Doubleday, published by Vallentine Mitchell & Co. Ltd, London 1952, reprinted by permission of the publisher. Excerpt from *Forgotten: A Sister's Struggle to Save Terry Anderson, America's Longest-held Hostage* by Peggy Say and Peter Knobler, published by Simon & Schuster 1991, reprinted by permission of Peggy Say. *Rescue Mission* © Anthony Masters 1994, (copyright material included is reprinted by permission of Nigel Marsh). Excerpt from *Louis Pasteur* by Madeleine P. Grant, published by Ernest Benn, London 1959, reprinted by permission of Curtis Brown.

Every effort has been made to obtain permission to reproduce copyright material but there may be cases where we have been unable to trace a copyright holder. The publisher will be happy to correct any omissions in future printings.